CASE STUDIES of
NORMAL ADOLESCENT GIRLS

ELSIE M. SMITHIES

ASSISTANT PRINCIPAL, UNIVERSITY HIGH SCHOOL
UNIVERSITY OF CHICAGO

NEW YORK   LONDON
D. APPLETON AND COMPANY

PRINTED IN THE UNITED STATES OF AMERICA

CASE STUDIES OF
NORMAL ADOLESCENT GIRLS

PREFACE

ALL those who have worked for any length of time with girls of high school age are aware that there are many adolescents who do not fall into the class of the abnormal but who are, nevertheless, poorly adjusted. That is to say, they have not learned how to live effectively, how to progress satisfactorily, or how to make happy and satisfying contacts with their everyday surroundings.

It is generally accepted by psychologists that the emotional life of adolescence is for the most part merely a continuance of the emotional trends that have developed during infancy and childhood. Yet because of the growing complexity of life at this period, the increasing awareness of self and the relation of self to others, adolescence often brings to a crisis and makes more acute and annoying factors which in childhood were accepted unquestioningly. Confusion ensues.

In many cases things are not what they seem. The outward reaction of a girl can be named easily but the cause of the reaction is remote and difficult to reach. Remedial work of even the simplest nature often cannot be undertaken until the underlying causes are discovered. With the hope of helping adolescent girls to a happier adjustment a technique named the case history method has been developed.

The procedure is not based on theory alone. It involves

the intimate personal contact with girls, teachers, educational experts, doctors and parents in order that there
may be made available competent first-hand information
on the history of the physical, mental, emotional, and
intellectual development of the girl who is studied.   All
factors in the home life, the school experiences, and social
contacts that may throw light on the problem are carefully
scrutinized.   Before the diagnosis is made there is careful
weighing and interpretation of the value of the materials
collected.   Thus through a scientific approach there is
ascertained a genuine understanding of attitudes and behavior; the surface evidence is penetrated, and the deeply
rooted causes of maladjustment are unearthed.

In this volume there has been a definite attempt to
make the technique as explicit as possible so that those
wishing to engage in case studies may have a guiding
method of approach.

The special cases reported have been chosen from a
storehouse of case work with adolescent girls.   They are
representative of the typical problems which are being
met repeatedly in the school and home situation—cases
of self-distrust, physical disability, exhibitionism, volitional retardation, depression, insecurity, parental domi-
nance and inferiority fear.

No case is fictitious.   Each of the studies presented is
the record of a real human being who was not functioning
in a way commensurate with her capacity, but who was
eager to behave as other people do, to accomplish as
others and to enjoy the normal contacts and pleasures of
girlhood.

The book is intended to be of service to five classes of
readers: All types of guidance officers working with girls

(deans, counselors, directors of religious education, leaders of groups in such organizations as Camp Fire Girls, Girl Scouts, Girl Reserves), classroom teachers, students in educational courses in the training of teachers, parents, the general reader who is interested in social problems.

The purpose of the book will have been accomplished if the reader turns from its pages more aware of the sensitivity of the adolescent, more sympathetic with the struggles encountered in the growing up process and more imbued with the spirit of Spinoza who said, "Neither ridicule, nor condemn, but try to understand."

Acknowledgment is made to Dr. Henry C. Morrison, whose profound knowledge, human understanding, and patient helpfulness have been a constant source of inspiration and encouragement.

E. M. S.

CONTENTS

CASE STUDIES OF NORMAL
ADOLESCENT GIRLS

CHAPTER I

THE TECHNIQUE OF CASE WORK

ADJUSTMENT of the individual to life lies at the basis of the philosophy of education to-day. In the last half century the difficulty of individual adjustment has increased in direct proportion to the growth of the complexity of our social and economic organization, to the development of monotonous routine and standardization in industry, to the tendency to mass production, and to the laxity resulting from social and moral freedom. More and more bewildering and perplexing to the child has become the growing-up process, more and more baffling the gradual and normal development away from the early infantile mechanisms of adjustment to the mature, balanced methods used in adulthood. The greater the standardization in social and economic life, the greater has become the need for concern in respect to the development of the individual pupil.

Because of the resulting confusion home and church have pushed into the province of the school problems which, heretofore, were not conceded as its responsibility. The school has been called upon to assume the task of the solution of individual difficulties not only in the scholastic field but also in emotional, social and moral realms.

Economic changes revolutionary in character have crowded the schools with vast enrollments and have brought under educational supervision a far greater variety of students. In consequence, the individual has been neglected. Not neglected, perhaps, in the teaching of subject matter, but certainly overlooked in the delicate and intimate adjustments of life.

In order to meet the various demands which have arisen and to satisfy the growing feeling that the school is one of the very best agencies to help the individual to solve his varied problems, educational thinking has broadened and expanded. Attention has been directed toward the scholastic problems of individual differences, to segregation of pupils according to ability, to extensive programs of extracurricular activities, to character education, and to vocational guidance.

As a result of this stimulation there have come into the school systems of this country all types of special guidance officers—the director of personnel, dean of girls, dean of boys, educational counselor, vocational counselor, visiting teacher, supervisor of health education, director of character education. The function of each of these officers is to give to each individual the specific guidance which he particularly needs to help him make the most satisfying and satisfactory adjustment to his environment.

Because of emergency situations, or community pressure, or the overenthusiastic zeal of administrators, many of these officers have been imposed, as it were, upon the established educational system without the adequate definition of duties or the proper demarcation of fields of work. Overlapping of function of these guidance officers has been wasteful, confusing and irritating. In most school systems the personnel work has been successful only because the various members of the staff have happened to agree temperamentally. When they have not been compatible, the result has been internal conflict and friction.

In spite of overlapping, friction and petty jealousies, the school through these guidance officers has handled admirably certain phases of adjustment. Difficulties common to all pupils have been well taken care of through group conferences, various types of girls' and boys' clubs, Big Sister and Big Brother schemes, sponsor organizations and home room plans. But it is very rare that actual individual difficulties have been studied. It is granted that most children find their way through school according to expectation. Yet every educator, whether in a large or small school, knows that he is daily confronted with cases of serious scholastic failure, of emotional maladjustment, of physical disorder or of social inadequacy, types of maladjustment so fundamental that there is need of individual attention and necessity for scientific pedagogical case work.

The argument has been and in many communities still is that this type of work is too expensive both in time and money. School budgets are too small. Yet the argument should have little validity. Is it economic wisdom to provide funds only for the correction of the mischief which has already been done? Communities, states and the nation are all pouring out vast sums for the upkeep of juvenile courts, detention homes, reformatories, jails, penitentiaries, sanitariums and asylums. Yet appropriations for the study of individual difficulties in their incipiency are denied. How long is preventive and corrective work in our schools to be considered educational waste?

There is little coöperative study of the individual with an expert in charge to see the individual as a whole. There is a crying need for the officer trained to gather materials, to weigh their values, to coördinate and correlate the findings, to pronounce a diagnosis, and to prescribe treatment for the pedagogical case problem. The difficulties of human relationship and adjustment are worthy of the same careful, scientific scrutiny and study as is being given physical adjustment to-day by the medical diagnostician.

To the later specialist, each patient is an individual case with certain hereditary susceptibilities, tendencies and definite individual reactions to exciting agencies. As a result the physical well-being of the patient is restored only by a thorough study of the patient from every possible angle.

In the same way the pedagogical case-worker, diagnostician in the educational field, must individualize his problems and by study of the pupil from every possible angle discover his peculiar susceptibilities, tendencies, reactions and fundamental disorders.

An enlightening analogy can be made to the work of the medical diagnostician and his relation to other experts in the same field. Although there are numerous specialists, such as X-ray and laboratory technicians, research workers, nurses, physicians of special organs, there is no serious overlapping of function. Each has his specific problem to investigate and the knowledge gained through the various contributory fields becomes the tool of the correlator, the diagnostician. He takes the essential findings of each specialist, interprets the data contributed in the light of the individual patient and as a result of the correlation makes his final decision or diagnosis.

Just so the educational diagnostician or pedagogical case-worker becomes the correlator of the materials and findings of the experts in various educational fields.

The diagram on page 8 will illustrate the comparison.

WHAT TYPE OF PROBLEM IS THE PROPERTY OF THE PEDAGOGICAL CASE-WORKER?

Every administrator is aware of the fact that our schools have in their enrollment young adolescents in every degree of maladjustment. He has observed the quiet, retiring youngster who does class work well but who is seclusive, unhappy, burdened and moody; the mean, jealous person who constantly creates disturbance in the group; the egocentric, superior, supercilious pupil who makes himself obnoxious and unpopular; the compensator who lies, steals and plays truant; the pupil of low mentality who cannot accomplish nor find satisfaction in academic work; and the pupil who has ability but who has trouble with learning due to all sorts of emotional upsets or to lack of sufficient preparation. This seething mass of misfits, striving each in his own way to gain the feeling of equality and the happiness of security, provides a great many problems. The competent school now has to assume the responsibility of teaching them not only academic subjects but also instructing them in how to behave, how to mingle with their fellows, and how to

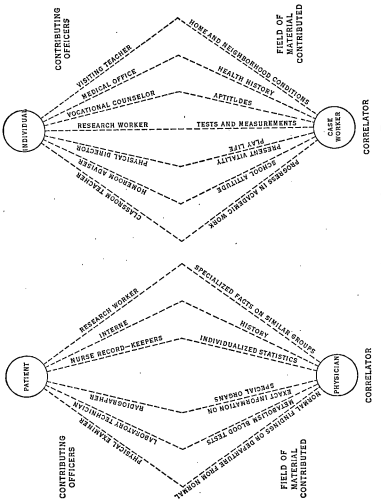

DIAGRAM OF ANALOGOUS FUNCTIONS OF MEDICAL AND PEDAGOGICAL DIAGNOSTICIAN

adapt themselves to the complex conditions of social and economic life.

The case-worker takes upon himself the task of scientifically seeking the information which will assist in the remedial work for those pupils who because of some defect or disturbance, either mental, physical or emotional, cannot study effectively, cannot make satisfying social contacts or cannot face the realities of life comfortably.

THE CASE-WORKER

What preparation is necessary to handle these problems?

Many psychiatrists to-day state that the tools of a medical adjustment worker are not so complex nor are the problems so intricate but that a great number of the cases which come to the offices of psychiatrists could easily have been handled in the school.

Doctor Bernard Glueck has stated: "In the large majority of maladjusted children who finally get to psychiatric clinics the problem is not one of psychopathology but that of a better understanding of the child. The outstanding element in the psychiatrist's equipment in an endeavor to understand the child is just an honest intent and desire to do so, coupled with a thoroughly open-minded and unbiased attitude toward each problem presented."[1] There is indeed nothing very complex about that. It is human sympathy and desire to help combined

---

[1] Bernard Glueck, *Some Extra-Curricular Problems of the Classroom,* Joint Committee on Methods of Preventing Delinquency, Publication No. 34 (50 East 42nd St., New York City).

with some scientific knowledge and some technical procedure of studying cases which is the whole equipment the case-worker needs.

First and foremost, the case-worker should be a teacher with good training and adequate experience in the principles and practices of teaching, with knowledge of the theory of education, and with some background in educational psychology. Inasmuch as the scientific study of an individual touches the whole horizon of human experience the work makes inroads into the contiguous territories of social service, medicine and psychiatry. The case-worker cannot, of course, be expected to be an expert in all these fields, but he should be aware of the problems and contributions of the specialists in them. The best preparation for the work will include special training and extensive reading relative to tests and measurement, nutrition work with children, mental and physical growth, principles of social work, medical and social psychiatry, and psychopathology.

Assuming that a case-worker has acquired the scientific and technical foundation and background required for effective diagnosing there are still certain characteristics which must be possessed to carry on pedagogical case work successfully:

1. The first requisite is common sense, that quality which gives balance in judgment of essentials and nonessentials and makes one realize when a case should go out from the jurisdiction of the school and be brought into contact with medical and psychiatric specialists.

2. One must like and understand people and must enjoy dealing with all types of individuals. Unless a worker has these qualities and can show them, case work will be but a cold, perfunctory and profitless procedure.

3. To evaluate the real character of another person and to discern what he may be trying to hide requires strong intuitive faculties.

4. Originality in questioning is most essential.

5. Keenness in detecting clews to a solution of the problem, alertness in following valid suggestions and accuracy in collecting data differentiate the expert from the novice.

6. One must be capable of not only compiling data but also of using and interpreting the compiled data intelligently.

7. A reasonably good memory is an asset for there will be need to carry accurately in one's mind the various details, clews and relationships of the different witnesses contributing to the investigation. Note-taking during a conference formalizes the procedure and is usually out of place.

8. The manner of speech and action of the worker should inspire confidence and create ease.

9. The worker must strive to be impersonal, unbiased and unemotional toward all facts and situations presented, as prejudice and undue sentimentality and emotion make the acquiring of information almost impossible and prove to be serious deterrents in interpreting the facts after they have been secured.

10. The art of being close-mouthed is the *sine qua non* of an efficient case-worker.

METHODS OF COLLECTING MATERIALS

1. *Individual Folder*

Adjustment in pupils is variable and inconstant because of the fluctuating reactions of an individual to his ever-changing environment. The pupil who is not a problem to-day may be poorly adjusted to-morrow. Adjustment is not static. Therefore, every case-worker should have easy of access a folder for each individual under his charge, and bit by bit he should accumulate the significant evidences of the changes and growth taking place in the pupil. Tardiness, frequent absence, failure in courses, misbehavior and a score of other items may seem to be of little significance at the time but when studied in connection with other factors or when viewed each in the light of the other, they may be full of meaning. The importance of keeping detailed information on each pupil cannot be overemphasized.

2. *The Personal Interview*

In the collecting of material the guidance officer is dependent to a great extent upon the personal interview. Executives in business, psychiatrists, physicians and social workers have all proved that the interview is an absolute necessity. In guidance work one may have secured much valuable evidence in the results of tests of physical fitness, of mental alertness, of emotional balance and of educational achievement. These remain, however, bare skeletons unless vitalized by a personal interview with the pupil. So much is at stake in these personal contacts that the utmost care must be used in planning them. First, if files and folders are to be used they must be easily accessible. Unless the case-worker has in his mind the purpose of the interview, it is very apt to become merely a haphazard conversation, pointless and wasteful. The conciseness of statement, the clearness of purpose, the careful weighing of evidence by the better judges in the courts is in sharp contrast to the dawdling, evasive, long drawn out pseudo-interviews practiced by many personnel workers.

The human equation is one of the most vital factors in

the interview. Each individual is a dynamic personality who is the product of his heredity, his background and his life experiences, the things which appeal to him and those things which antagonize him. The personality of each individual plays upon the other. Until *rapport* has been established there is little chance to proceed with the collecting of materials. Laird says that the ideal attitude in establishing the right atmosphere seems to be one of quiet understanding with avoidance of emotional tone, but evidence of friendly interest. A feeling of comfortableness, security and trust must be present to warrant even the first steps toward discovering the basis of the real trouble.

The choice of the time and place of the interview is exceedingly important. Postponement, even indefinitely, is usually preferable to an attempt to adjust matters under unfavorable circumstances. Absolute privacy, some semblance of comfortableness and quiet are the requisites of the place. In selecting the time both the worker and the pupil must be considered. When will there be the least fatigue on the part of both? When will the attention of each be least absorbed in other tasks or pleasures? When will there be the least hurry, worry and nervous tension on the part of each? These are the elements which can make or break the interview.

The aim of the interview should be to find out what is working underneath, what is the real trouble, what is the pupil's own story? Usually the problem pupil has a surface and a buried story. To the ordinary observer he presents an exterior which is misleading and completely conceals the fundamental difficulty. The hidden story of the personal difficulty must be brought to the surface.

At intervals there will be clews of the inner story breaking through into the surface story. The case-worker should be alert to all these clews as they appear. Furthermore, there should be, at times, definite stimulation and the use of all sorts of incentives to reach the climax by presentation of facts which one knows will bring certain responses and further clews. The pupil must be permitted to talk himself out so that the hidden story may at last reach the surface one.

ADMONITIONS TO INTERVIEWERS

1. A cross-examination attitude gets nowhere. An interview which consists of prescribed questions and answers is obviously a crude affair and does not yield the hidden story which is ascertained indirectly rather than as a result of direct interrogation. Avoid "grilling."

2. One must be patient, painstaking and slow to advance for there is no short cut to results. Dr. Miriam Van Waters says: [2] "Of all facts known to social workers about human life, facts which deal with changing human behavior yield up their secrets with the most reluctance."

3. Avoid sentimentality. The sympathetic attitude must not be carried so far as to distort the judgment of the worker or to make him incapable of getting at the facts of the case.

4. Helen Myrick says: "The person at all times during the interview must be looked upon as an individual. He is not an inanimate object who is to be worked upon by the expert. The interview should be a dialogue in its true sense, not a 'sales-talk monologue.'"

5. The mere passing over the threshold of an office often causes a pupil's behavior to be far from normal. This is particularly true if the interview tends to be of an inquisitional

---

[2] *Youth in Conflict*, p. 178.

character.. Reactions under such circumstances are seldom true indications of what might happen under more natural conditions.

6. In this interplay of human personalities the law of instinctive imitation is very active. The same emotion which is observed in the worker is very apt to be awakened within the pupil. If the former is angry, calm or cheerful the same quality is apt to come out in the interviewee.

7. Beware of prejudice. It is a well-known fact that previous associations of physical and mental characteristics definitely affect the impressions made by the pupil upon the case-worker. That is to say, the worker must be constantly on guard against the human tendency of association of some mannerism, some feature, certain type of posture or some external peculiarity in *another* person with the same mannerism in the *new* person being interviewed. This law, known as conditioned reactions, if not recognized will seriously affect the results of the interview.

8. The first and hardest lesson to learn about people is that one who needs help can be helped only if he wants to be helped. There is no such thing as making an adjustment for somebody else.

9. At no time should the pupil be labeled a problem.

3. *Witnesses*

In the complete investigation of any problem the worker must come in contact with agencies and individuals outside of the province of the school. This contact is fraught with difficulty and must be made with the utmost care and discretion. Because of the frailties of human nature the mere mention of any difficulty connected with an individual can cause flights of imagination, maligning scandal and pernicious gossip in many witnesses. This is particularly true if the case-worker carelessly throws out suggestions or resorts to leading questions. Evidence gained from such sources must be censored and discounted accordingly.

4. *The Staff Conference*

Before the investigation is brought to a close and a final diagnosis can be made the case-worker will have conferences with his coworkers, the visiting teacher, the classroom teacher, the homeroom adviser, the medical officer, in fact with all the officers from contributing fields. Taken apart, the findings of each person concerned with the case may have little value or significance. In co-operating consultation this group should sift the evidence in order to evaluate the validity of the contributions.

The author has found the following suggestions valuable in weighing the authenticity of the information secured: [8]

Critique of Evidence as a Whole

1. If a teacher cites a learning difficulty, what is the character of that person's teaching? (Teachers often impute defects to pupils when the defect is their own.)
2. Does the testimony of the witnesses in the case hang together?
   a. Teachers?
   b. Principals?
   c. Parents?
   d. Child?
   e. Outside agencies?
3. Does evidence run by types of teaching or by certain teachers?
4. What is competent evidence inside or outside of school and what ought to be excluded?

---

[3] Henry C. Morrison, lecture, 1926.

A guide in sifting evidence:
1. Opinion versus fact
2. Hearsay versus first-hand information
3. Inference versus fact
4. Is the witness trying to make a case?
5. Has the witness an emotional attitude toward the case?
6. Is the witness testifying to facts within his competency?

WHAT MATERIAL SHOULD BE COLLECTED?

Dr. Richard Cabot in speaking of medical cases says: "Cases do not often come to us systematically arranged like the account of typhoid in a textbook of 'Practice of Medicine.' They are usually presented to us from an angle and with one symptom, generally the misleading one, in the foreground. From this point of view we must reason our way back into the inner processes and more obscure causes which guide our therapeutic work."

In the same scientific way in pedagogical case work the school must push beyond the misleading surface symptoms to the real causes of the difficulty.

Any given individual to be studied is the result of the interplay of heredity, that is, a biologic resemblance to his progenitors, his environment and his reaction to it, and acquired characteristics which are partly dependent upon the environment and upon the natural step-up or step-down in the evolutionary scale of which the individual is a minute but necessary part.

The author has used the following outline for ten years as a guide in securing the factors in heredity and environment which have been operative in making the individual what he is to-day.

STUDY OF ....

I. DESCRIPTION OF THE CASE AS PRESENTED

II. INVESTIGATION OF PRESENT SCHOOL LIFE

A. *Scholastic Record*
1. Discovery of difficulties and successes through records and teachers' estimates
2. Scores and analyses of tests
   a. Mental tests (language and non-language)
   b. Reading tests (comprehension and rate)
   c. Vocabulary tests
   d. Arithmetic tests (fundamental operations and problems with and without numbers)
   e. Apperceptive mass

B. *Present Physical Condition*
1. Defects
   a. Hearing
   b. Seeing
   c. Breathing
   d. Coördination
2. Any permanent effects of illnesses or operations?
3. Any tendency toward
   a. Colds?
   b. Sore throat?
   c. Indigestion?
   d. Nervousness?
   e. Persistent constipation?
4. Any marked physical weakness?

C. *Social Record in School*
1. Participation in school activities, *e.g.,* clubs, dances, athletics, etc.
2. Number, age, type of friends
3. Adjustments to fellow students

D. *Composite Personality Scale* (based on the estimates of five or more people)

	High		Medium		Low	
Refined						Coarse
Modest						Vain
Democratic						Snobbish
Cheery						Peevish
Patient						Irritable
Courteous						Discourteous
Friendly						Reserved
Cordial						Indifferent
Sociable						Unsociable
Imaginative						Prosaic
Altruistic						Selfish
Coöperative						Combative
Open-to-sugges- tion						Opinionated
Optimistic						Pessimistic
Contented						Dissatisfied
Keenly alive						Apathetic
Loquacious						Taciturn
Self-poised						Flighty
Calm						Excitable
Trustful						Jealous
Well-spoken						Gossipy
Common-sense						Lacking in judgment
Frank						Underhanded
Honest						Dishonest
Reliable						Unreliable
Reasonable						Unreasonable
Prompt						Dilatory
Industrious						Idle
Attentive						Inattentive
Steady						Intermittent

   E. *Parents' Version of the Difficulty*
   F. *Pupil's Version of the Difficulty*
   G. *Interpretation of the Findings*

III. INVESTIGATION OF LIFE OUTSIDE OF SCHOOL

   A. *Meals*
      1. Regularity
      2. Eating
      3. Dietary quality

B. *Sleep*
    1. Number of hours
    2. Type (restful, restless, dreaming)

C. *Exercise*
    1. Type?
    2. Alone or with companion?
    3. Effect (stimulating, enervating)

D. *Home Life*
    1. Manner of living (house, apartment, hotel)
    2. Cultural facilities
    3. Number of children in the home
    4. Outsiders in the home (grandparents, uncles, aunts, boarders, or servants)
    5. Pupil's reaction to
        a. Brothers and sisters
        b. Mother
        c. Father
        d. Other members of the household
    6 Reaction of each member of the household upon the others
    7. Is there any evidence of favoritism?

E. *Social Diversions*
    1. Type
    2. Frequency
    3. Type of companions

F. *Interpretation of the Findings*

IV. EARLY HISTORY AND DEVELOPMENT

A. *Family History*
    1. Father
        a. History of father's family
            i. Any cancer, goiter or tuberculosis for three generations of blood relatives?
            ii. Any member who was a hard drinker?
        b. Personal
            i. Father's present age
            ii. Age of father at ....'s birth
               Previous children
               Age interval
               Subsequent children and age interval

        iii. Present business
        iv. Education
            (a) Grammar school
            (b) High school
            (c) Advanced
            (d) College
        v. Interests outside the home
    c. Discussion and conclusion

2. Mother
    a. History of mother's family
        i. Any cancer, goiter, tuberculosis for three generations of blood relatives?
        ii. Any member who was a hard drinker?
    b. Personal
        i. Mother's present age
        ii. Age of mother when married
        iii. Age of mother at birth of first child
        iv. Birth number of ....
        v. Education
            (a) Grammar school
            (b) High school
            (c) Advanced
            (d) College
        vi. Interests outside the home (club life, recreation, philanthropies)
    c. Discussion and conclusion

B. *Physical History of Child*

1. Pregnancy—duration
2. Birth of child
    a. Delivery
    b. Weight of child at birth
    c. Method of feeding
3. Early childhood
    a. At what age she walked
    b. At what age she talked
    c. At what age first tooth appeared
    d. General health
    e. Diseases of childhood

C. *Emotional History of Child*
  1. Fears, anxiety
  2. Tantrums
  3. Shyness
  4. Delinquencies (lying, stealing)
  5. Conclusions

D. *Scholastic History of Child*
  1. Types of schools attended (progressive, private, or conventional public)
  2. Equipment of schools
  3. Type of instructors (progressive or conservative)
  4. Location of schools
  5. Grading system used in schools
  6. Record of scholarship in previous schools
      a. Any marked disability?
      b. Any marked ability?
      c. Any double promotions?
      d. Any failures to be promoted?
      e. Any evidence of resentment, dropping off of interest, anger, sullenness?
      f. Any periods of absence? Cause?
  7. Attitude toward
      a. Companions
      b. Teachers
      c. Parents
  8. Conclusions

E. *Interpretation of Findings*

V. GENERAL DIAGNOSIS OF THE CASE

VI. TREATMENT AND PROGNOSIS

THE DIAGNOSIS

The real test of a case-worker is the diagnosis of the problem. The laborious, tedious, painstaking collection of material in the history has but one purpose and goal, namely, the finding of the root of the whole difficulty so that remedial work may be administered. Before commencing the diagnosis the worker should feel confident that all facts accumulated are authentic, that every field has been thoroughly investigated and that a sufficient check has been given to all data. In unraveling this intricate tangle of facts one must never lose track of the individual and his susceptibility to particular reactions. In emotional cases, especially, it does not seem to be a certain cause alone which creates trouble but rather a specific cause in a particular person at a particular time. The identical cause can be found in many other individuals without apparent distress. If, however, a disturbance has resulted, it is indicative that the individual was not able to compensate adequately and sufficiently at the time to take the sting, so to speak, out of the cause. Therefore, in that specific person a serious maladjustment has taken place which has continued to act as a definite inhibitory factor in development.

The diagnosis has four steps: (1) the critical scrutiny and interpretation of the evidence found in each field covered in the history; (2) the logical relation of each fact to the other; (3) the weighing of their mutual values, and (4) the unifying of the findings into a definite disorder with fundamental and contributory causations. Until the fundamental causes have been discovered and removed by treatment permanent cure cannot be assured.

Doctor Henry C. Morrison defines the diagnosis as a reasoned inference from data which have been accumulated. To quote:

A critical point is to distinguish between *cause* and *occasion*. The whole purpose of the case history is to find the occasion. The *occasion* is past history and is what started it all. *Causation* is some kind of inhibition still present in the child.

The primary causation is the condition within the pupil which is inferred on evidence to be at the root of the whole matter and which if eliminated will open the way for readjustment.

Out of the primary grows the secondary. The secondary is a consequence of the primary, but is itself operating as causation. Out of the secondary grows the tertiary and so on. Primary causation may result in multiple secondary causations. Causation which is outside of the main chain of primary, secondary, tertiary, etc., is contributory causation.[4]

. The application of the principles of case work is restricted in this book to cases of girls of high-school age who have had difficulties which could not be removed by the ordinary procedure of school administration. The technique in Case I is given in great detail to illustrate the exact method used in arriving at a diagnosis of the difficulty and in determining the type of treatment to be given to the individual. Case II represents the study of a superior student with no scholastic difficulties and is used as a basis for comparison and contrast with Case I. It must be borne in mind that all names used in the manuscript are fictitious. Furthermore in some places the facts have been slightly disguised without impairing the essential veracity and significance of the narrative.

It is the sincere hope of the author that these cases representing different types of difficulties may serve as helpful guides to those who are interested in the study of adjustment of pupil problems.

---

[4] Henry C. Morrison, lectures, 1926.

CHAPTER II

SELF-DISTRUST: THE CASE OF
GRETCHEN KREUTZ

GRETCHEN KREUTZ, whose case is reported in this study, was a member of the sophomore class in a cosmopolitan, midwestern high school. She was fifteen years and six months of age. At the beginning of this study she was enrolled in Latin IA, English II, ancient history, and general science.

Gretchen's case came to the attention of the worker during the third week after the opening of school. She was reported by her science instructor as having difficulty. This report was considered to be of a more serious nature than a first report, so early in the year, ordinarily would be, because during her freshman year Gretchen had carried science until March of that year. At that time, after conference with her first science instructor, it was decided that she should drop science, for she was so far behind that it seemed impossible for her to make up the work and carry three other subjects. This second failure, therefore, demanded immediate investigation.

INVESTIGATION OF PRESENT SCHOOL LIFE

Her present science instructor said that he had explained points over and over to her with apparently no satisfactory results in her comprehension of the material. She appeared to feel a little above the class because of her age and looked upon the rest of the class as babies, while she was a young lady. On two occasions, however, she had shown interest enough to remain after class and complete some work she was doing. In class she attended to her work and asked questions when necessary.

Although Gretchen had studied Latin for one year, she had made no real progress. She was in a special class which was composed of a group of slow workers who were permitted to go as fast as they were able. An evidence of slowness that was perfectly clear in class, but which could not be submitted in black and white, was reaction-time from stimulus to response when a word she did not know was presented, *i.e.*, when she did know and got it right the time was longer than in any cases with which the teacher had ever dealt. In the Latin class, Gretchen was attentive, but with passive attention. She never seemed to put up a real fight to get things.

In ancient history, too, Gretchen was not meeting with much success, for, as her instructor stated, she was well-meaning but had not formed habits of study. She had no power of sustained application and with difficulty grasped the meaning of the material which she was reading. Her notebook work was crude and ill-formed, corresponding to her ideas, and her written work was of the same type. She found it difficult to focus her thoughts, as appeared in her answers to questions and in her oral responses.

A study of the sustained-application profile in history showed constant interruption of her own thoughts, as if she did not quite understand what she was doing. It was to be noted especially that she was working most of the time, but it was not purposeful study. She spent a few minutes on the notes, another few minutes reading the book, and then a few minutes writing, then back to the notes. It was significant that she was not disorderly. There was no whispering or playing with her neighbors, although she was restless.

Gretchen's instructor in English reported that she was having a little difficulty in her written expression, due to lack of mastery of elementary usage. She was applying herself very well and her attitude was most commendable. Whenever she was given a paper to rewrite, she attacked the task with determination to make it a better paper.

An attention profile was taken also during her library period. It showed three or four periods of distraction in each of the separate twenty-minute periods taken on three different days. Gretchen was reading a book for English and never seemed to get really interested in it. Her behavior was exemplary, for she never spoke to any one, nor disturbed her table mates. Yet her application was only partial. Gretchen never became so absorbed that she shut out completely other stimuli about her.

The above evidence points to difficulties in learning in Latin, in science, in history, and in the mechanics of English composition; that is to say, the trouble is general. There is a pronounced lesson-learning attitude.[1] Gretchen has an interest in school and in her own success, as is shown in staying after class to complete work in science, in asking questions for help, and in eagerness to improve

---

[1] Henry C. Morrison, *The Practice of Teaching in the Secondary School* (The University of Chicago Press, second edition, 1931).

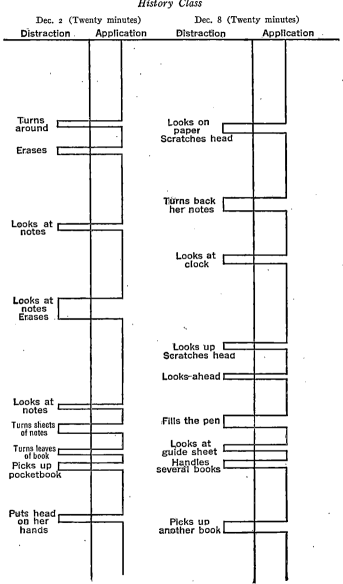

CHICAGO SUSTAINED APPLICATION PROFILE

History Class

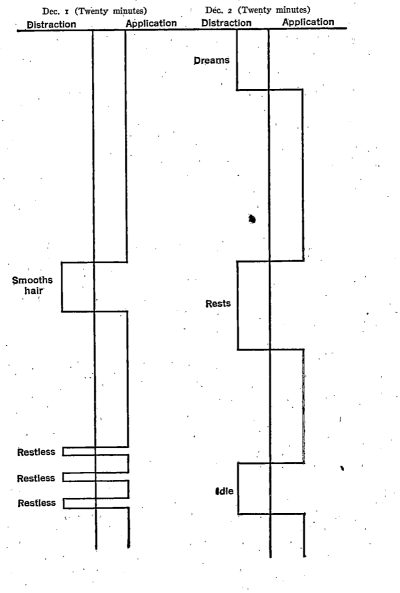

CHICAGO-SUSTAINED APPLICATION PROFILE
Study Period

Dec. 1 (Twenty minutes)   Dec. 2 (Twenty minutes)
Distraction   Application   Distraction   Application

Dreams

Smooths
hair

Rests

Restless

Restless

Idle

Restless

her English papers. Her sustained application profiles both in history and in study indicate partial, apathetic attention.

Tests

Mental Tests.—Three intelligence tests were given to Gretchen: the Terman Group Tests of Mental Ability, Thurstone Psychological Tests, and the Army Beta Test. The first two are language tests, the last nonlanguage:

Test	*Result*
Terman .......I.Q. 94	
Thurstone .....(78 attempts, 58 correct	
	4 percentile rank in Sophomore Class)
Army Beta ....High Average C+	

An analysis of the tests showed that scores were lowered by certain definite types of questions and that there was no evidence of mental weakness.

ANALYSIS OF TERMAN GROUP TESTS OF MENTAL ABILITY

Test	Number Correct	Number Attempted
Information	10	17
Best Answer	8	8
Word Meaning	21	26
Logical Selection	13	16
Arithmetic	3	7
Sentence Meaning	13	19
Analogies	13	13
Mixed Sentences	11	12
Classification	13	15
Number Series	3	7

From a survey of the above scores it can be seen that the results on information tests, arithmetic problems, and number series are the weak spots. It is quite evident that her I.Q. 94 and her mental age, 14 years, 11 months, do not represent her native wit. She failed on such questions as "Confucius founded the Chinese religion," a type of thing which one gets from wide contacts in reading and not from native ability, either directly or by implication. The arithmetic difficulty is also something which does not show lack of intelligence, but lack of training.

RESULTS OF THURSTONE PSYCHOLOGICAL TEST

	Number Correct	Number Wrong	Number Attempted
Gretchen's score	58	20	78
Sophomore			
Quartile 1	75.3	(75 per cent of class received this score or above)	
Median	88.1	(50 per cent of class received this score or above)	
Quartile 3	101.3	(25 per cent of class received this score or above)	
Freshman			
Quartile 1	66.3		
Median	79.1		
Quartile 3	90.1		
Grade VIII			
Quartile 1	57.7		
Median	65.3		
Quartile 3	74.0		

The total number of attempts in Gretchen's test is about the same as the number *correct* in the *lowest* quartile of the sophomore class. Gretchen's score is about equal to the lowest quartile of the eighth grade class. The number of her *attempts* is just about equal to the number *correct* in the *highest quartile* of the grade.

ANALYSIS OF THURSTONE PSYCHOLOGICAL TEST

Test	Number Correct	Number Attempted
Informational Questions	10	18
True-false	7	9
Identical Meanings	5	9
Completion of English Sentences	9	10
Number Series	10	11
Relationship	18	20

The greatest weakness on this test was information questions, with identical meanings in the second place.

On the nonlanguage test (Army Beta) the answers were very good except on tests 2 and 7. Both of these questions test space perception. She failed outright in the problem of fitting geometrical figures into a square. In test 2, when she was required to count blocks piled one on the other, she saw nothing but a flat surface. Even with failure on two out of seven tests, she ranked on this test high average in intelligence.

From the evidence given on the intelligence tests, defect in mentality can be eliminated as a factor in Gretchen's maladjustment.

Reading Tests.—A battery of tests was given to Gretchen in which she scored as shown in the table.

The Gray Oral showed a very high rate of speed with fewer errors than the average.

In the Thorndike-McCall test, which is a reading-study test, she missed but three of making a perfect score. These errors were in the last part of the test, which is difficult. She gave correct answers consistently through the first thirty-two questions.

The results on the Van Wagenen reading tests showed ability to read materials of various types. She was about average in the science and literature type and a little below in the history.

RESULTS OF READING TESTS

Test	Gretchen's Score	Norm for Grade	Percentile Rank (Relative Position in a group of 100)
Gray Oral Tests			
Rate	47 per cent	56.0 per cent	91.0
Quality	5 errors	5.9 errors	63.0
Thorndike-McCall Reading			
Scale (Form F)	33	30	95.0
Van Wagenen Reading Scale			
Science	82	82.7	51
Literature	83	82.0	41
History	81	85.0	43
Burgess Silent Reading Scale			
(P. S. 1)	12		

The Burgess Silent Reading Test was given to Gretchen alone and her reactions were watched closely. She read the directions, executed the orders, and asked no questions. She made a score of twelve, which is fifty-six per cent for the eighth grade. (In terms of school grades promoted, Gretchen was in the tenth grade.) She attempted only twelve. Her movements while taking the test were slow, deliberate, and apparently with thorough understanding. In fact, in all the tests which were given, Gretchen read the directions and got to work immediately without asking questions. She showed good ability to interpret instructions.

All tests gave evidence that Gretchen could read, that she had a notion of what reading was for, and that she read as understandingly as the average, although she might read rather slowly in some types of work.

In connection with the giving of tests, a very interest-

DETAILED RESULTS OF REAVIS-BRESLICH DIAGNOSTIC TESTS IN THE FUNDAMENTAL OPERATIONS OF ARITHMETIC AND IN PROBLEM SOLVING

Test	Number Attempted	Correct Number	Time Given, Minutes	Median, VII A	Median, VIII A
Tests I—VIII					
Addition		2	3		
Subtraction		4	1.5		
Multiplication		5	3		
Division		3	4		
Addition and Subtraction of Fractions...		1	2		
Multiplication and Division of Fractions		5	2		
Placing Decimal Point in Multiplication ..		8	1		
Placing Decimal Point in Division		8	1.5		
Score: I—VIII		36		32.21	38.53
Test IX Problems without Numbers	8	1	6	3.20	4.42
Test X Problems with Numbers	9	7	4	7.25	8.16

ing and perhaps significant thing occurred. When the worker was giving the first reading tests to Gretchen, she said, "I don't mind taking any kind of tests as long as you do not give me an arithmetic test. I hate arithmetic and cannot do it." For this reason the worker deemed it advisable to have a regular mathematics instructor give her a diagnostic test which she could do aloud and alone with him. The following report came back: "Gretchen understands the work. She does the work with confidence and with correct methods. There is nothing the matter with her arithmetic."

Arithmetic Tests.—The worker, being a little dubious, had her write the Reavis-Breslich Diagnostic Tests in the Fundamental Operations of Arithmetic and in Problem Solving. Close observation showed that while she was doing the problems in addition, it was necessary for her to count on her fingers and to put down the number to be carried to the next column.

In three minutes she was able to do but three problems in addition—one of which was incorrect—yet in her work on the multiplication problems she made no mistakes in addition.

Test IX is the most illuminating. It is clear that she did not think through a situation at all. She used the word multiply for subtract; in fact, the ideas multiply, divide, and subtract were all confused in her mind. In one situation she said "divide" and in the same type of problem the second time she said "subtract." It is clear that she did not recognize mathematical situations and did not know when her answers were absurd.

In problems with numbers she made two errors, one in which she did not recognize the problem at all, and the other in multiplication.

EXAMPLE

1. *Problem:* My milk bill was $3.20 last month. I pay 8 cents a pint. How many gallons of milk did I use last month?

Gretchen's answer:

$$\begin{array}{r} \$3.20 \\ 8 \\ \hline 25.60 \text{ gallons} \end{array}$$

2. *Problem:* $.45 \times 2 = ?$

$$\begin{array}{r} .45 \\ 2 \\ \hline .70 \end{array}$$

The problems involving fractions were practically all wrong. She added in every case of subtraction.

At the close of the above test a rapid card drill on multiplication was given. For the most part the responses seemed automatic, but there were several slips.

$$11 \times 6 = 56$$
$$2 \times 12 = 24, \text{ then } 36$$
$$8 \times 12 = 96 \text{ (after much hesitation)}$$
$$12 \times 7 = 62, \text{ then } 84$$

Gretchen had definite disabilities in mathematics. She had not learned to recognize mathematical situations with or without actual numbers. There was a little weakness in number combinations as shown in addition and rapid-fire multiplication tests. Work in fractions was exceedingly poor. It might have been concluded that Gretchen could recognize mathematical situations and do arithmetical processes when she was with an instructor and when she spoke them aloud, but the worker herself gave her multiplication and addition and had her do the problems aloud and the results were practically the same as when she wrote them.

Apperceptive Mass.—In the Ruch-Popenoe General Science Test, Gretchen made a score of 34.5 (median, 33).

In the Inglis Tests of English Vocabulary her score

was 50 (median, 63). An analysis of the test was as follows:

Page	Possible Score	Number Attempted	Number Correct
Page 1	50	36	21
Page 2	50	38	16
Page 3	50	22	13

A study of the answers in the Inglis test shows no specific weakness in any one field of English vocabulary.

STENQUIST MECHANICAL APTITUDE TEST

Test	Gretchen's Score	Median for Boys	Gretchen's Percentile Rank
Test I	33	42	23
Test II	16	37	4

Her score on Test I showed that Gretchen could fit parts together by observation. Her rank was in the lowest quartile for boys of her age. (There are no norms for girls.)

Test II demands more than the mere fitting of parts together. It requires in addition analysis of the parts to be fitted. Gretchen's score on this test was practically a negligible quantity. Her percentile rank is 4. Subjects which require a mechanical background would without doubt be most difficult for her.

Gretchen was a little below her grade in vocabulary and was exceedingly weak in mechanical background. The previous reports on the Terman Group Intelligence Test and the Thurstone Psychological examination suggest a weakness in general information.

The background which Gretchen had gained through her reading was narrow, for, although she had read voluminously, her books had been limited to girls' series, detective stories, and novels with fast-moving, exciting plots with little information or description.

Downey Will-Temperament Test.—A study of the profile made by the Downey Will-Temperament Test revealed some significant facts. Low scores on speed of movement, freedom from load, motor impulsion and flexibility, indicated that Gretchen could not work at her highest speed, that she took a long time to warm up to a task, that she had difficulty in adjusting herself, and had little ease in removing inhibitions. Her low score in volitional perseveration was a real weakness. Volitional perseveration involves the setting of oneself a problem. It is subjective initiative, that is, the willingness to keep at a task because the subject has set a goal for herself.

Far more instructive than the profile of the test were the reactions of the subject while she was taking the test. Traits in pairs of opposites were checked. Gretchen checked one of each pair rapidly without hesitation until she came to "inferior intelligence—superior intelligence." Then she hesitated, showed much confusion, and said to herself several times, "Oh, oh, I don't know whether I'm inferior or superior." Next, under her breath, she said with determination, "Well, I'm just going to check *superior.*"

Again, at the close of the test she was given an opportunity to change any of the characteristics which she had checked at the beginning. Her response was, "I don't need to recheck any except the one about intelligence. I don't know whether I am inferior or superior."

This hesitation in decision was not due to modesty, because she checked superiority in character without hesitation and without comment. The traits which she said that she was most confident of possessing in a marked degree are ambition, enthusiasm, *self-distrust,* orderliness, and cheerfulness. In this list there appears the same element of lack of confidence which was seen in her effort to decide whether she was inferior or superior in intelligence.

Further evidence that there was some weakness in automatic response in multiplication tables was given in this test, when she had to write her name and count by three's. Her first trial was: "3, 6, 9, 12, *14*—No, oh, what is it?— 18, 21, 24, 27, *31.*" Her second trial: "3, 6, 9, 12, 15, 17, 20, 24, 27."

Present Physical Condition

A thorough physical examination revealed no defects in hearing and only slight astigmatism of the right eye. Glasses were not recommended by the physician. A study of her reactions in gymnasium work, such as marching tactics, esthetic dancing, and work on the horses, gave every evidence of neuromuscular coördination. There were not, nor had there ever been, defects of speech.

Her height was 1.8 inches below the average height for her age and sex, and her weight was between nine and ten pounds below normal.

The examination of teeth showed a good condition except for malocclusion, which was being corrected.

Her health in general was good, but recommendations were made by the physician for periodic examination of the throat and thyroid. The tonsils were hypertrophied.

There was an old history of thyroid trouble and a goiter was still palpable. History of dysmenorrhea was evident.

Mother's Story

From all reports, Gretchen's behavior at home was exemplary, and she seemed to be living a normal life for a girl of her age. Her mother reported that she was happy, interested and lively at home at this time, for school was much nicer this year.

Pupil's Version of the Difficulty

When Gretchen appeared for a conference with the worker, her first remark was, "Has Mr. ——— (history instructor) sent me a poor report? If he has I shall never go home. I'm too ashamed." She showed genuine relief when she was assured that no report was to be sent home. This is good evidence of a lesson-learning attitude. Her absorbing interest was in the reports which were to be sent home. She was, however, distressed when she heard of her work in all her classes. "I'm trying very hard," she said, "but I have always been dumb in school, but (she quickly added) not out of school. I'm surprised I'm not doing well now, because this is the only year I have ever known anything or felt that I knew as much as other people. I came back to school this year with my mind made up to ask questions because other girls seem to be able to ask questions and not look *dumb,* and the teachers don't kill them, either. I like school, too, this year." The above shows that Gretchen was not aware of any study situation. She was setting up a great number of symptoms to demonstrate the fact that she was not dumb. Her lesson-learning attitude was completely developed.

Gretchen had been trying eagerly to get a report card saying that she was improving. Every day for a week she came into the office of the worker to ask if her good report had come yet. One day when the worker asked her why she was so eager, she answered, "I want the folks at home to know that I *can* do good work and don't *have* to fail." When the card finally arrived, her brother paid her a dollar and a half as a reward. Gretchen assured the worker that she didn't work for the money, because she did not know that she was going to get it.

Interpretation

The results of the numerous examinations showed that Gretchen worked constantly under a load with little drive, had little ability to remove inhibitions, and had practically no subjective initiative as was indicated by the Downey-Will Temperament Test. An ingrained inhibiting lack of confidence in her own ability seemed to go hand in hand with passive and only partial attention in study to cause difficulty in any or all subjects. The lesson-learning attitude of both Gretchen and the home was marked in the report card incident. Gretchen worked for commendation, not knowledge. Specific weakness in arithmetic, a defective background in mechanical devices and a lack of ideational background could well have accounted for her difficulty in science. The lack of a goodly store of general information contributed its share to Gretchen's poor work in English, and the lesson-learning attitude, with its tendency to compromise with the situation, could easily have accounted for Gretchen's lack of success in Latin.

Her apperceptive background seemed to be well-rounded, but rather meager.

INVESTIGATION OF LIFE OUTSIDE OF SCHOOL

Gretchen was a member of a family in comfortable circumstances. During her whole life she had lived in apartments located in the good residential neighborhoods of a large city. A visit to the home verified the worker's opinion that she was well brought up. There was every evidence of refinement and good background in both the father and the mother. Good books were plentiful in the library and showed that they had been used. Gretchen had always loved to read, and most of her evenings have been spent in that form of recreation. From early childhood she has been accustomed to the use of both public and home libraries. She also has had her own books.

The other member of the family was Brother Bob, a graduate of a well-known medical school in the East, now a prosperous young physician.

A canvass of her diet brought out some significant data. A girl of her age and activity requires from 2,300 to 2,600 calories a day. A careful record of Gretchen's food intake was kept over a period of seven days. In the computation of number of calories consumed, the worker allowed generously for inaccuracies. The average number of calories for the seven days was 1,075 daily. On two days her intake was only 675 and 855 calories respectively. She ate no breakfast, so it would have been very difficult for her to get the requisite amount of nourishment.

COMPARISON OF ACTUAL AND REQUIRED FOOD INTAKE

Food Element	Gretchen's Intake	Required Intake
Protein	38 grams	65-75 grams
Calcium	.62 of day's need	1.00
Phosphorus	.43 of day's need	1.00
Iron	6 milligrams	15 milligrams
Vitamin A	+ + +	+ + +
Vitamin B	+ +	+ + +
Vitamin C	+	+ + +

Gretchen's intake was low in every respect but Vitamin A. There was sufficient evidence that she was not taking enough food to give her energy for school work.

From early childhood Gretchen had felt inferior to the older brother. At an early age before she went to school, Gretchen confided to a friend of her mother's that Bob was the "whole thing" around their house. He couldn't do anything wrong. The boy was the first and only baby in eight years among all the relations. He was bright, did exceedingly well in school, and graduated from the grammar school at twelve. Gretchen felt he was "smart" and "brainy." An intimate friend of the family reported to the mother that Gretchen felt a little resentment in addition to the fact that she felt inferior.

In order to verify the mother's report concerning the above, the worker asked Gretchen casually, "Has your brother graduated from college?" Gretchen promptly answered, "Oh, yes. He is brilliant. He is the lily of the family. He is only twenty-four years old and he has been out of college for two years." The worker laughed and Gretchen continued, "He is perfect. He has never done a wrong thing in his life." The worker suggested:

"And Gretchen?" She finished the sentence: "—has never done anything right. He is eight years older than I am—I was an afterthought."

Gretchen seemed to lead a normal social life for a girl of her age. She had many friends and seemed to make social contacts easily. She had always enjoyed playing games and sports outside of school, but not in school.

Her vacations had been spent in short trips to several large cities, a few weeks in a summer resort, and a visit on a farm with several fine, wholesome girls.

During one period of her life she had had a girl friend who was frivolous, boy-crazy, and Charleston-mad. Gretchen spent as much of her spare time as she was permitted with this friend at her rooms in a neighboring hotel. Her one interest in life then was the Charleston, for as she said, "It made me forget." The friendship was eventually broken off and the mother felt that a bad influence had been removed.

Gretchen had a few responsibilities in the home, such as cleaning up her room in the morning, doing errands for her mother, setting and clearing the table, and washing the dishes on Thursday and Sunday when the maid was out.

Interpretation

There is every evidence that Gretchen was not getting enough calories in her daily diet to keep up her energy and to give to her a forceful physical drive.

The brightness of the older brother, his exalted place in the immediate family and among the relatives, and the fact that the bright child was the man-child, created in Gretchen an inferiority feeling of discouragement.

EARLY HISTORY AND DEVELOPMENT

Both Gretchen's paternal and maternal grandparents were German, and lived in Germany. The grandfathers were both of the merchant class and fairly well educated. Mrs. Kreutz was a high-school graduate; Mr. Kreutz a high-school and engineering school graduate, who had been a successful business man.

Physical History

Gretchen was the younger of two children, with a gap of eight years between the two. The mother reported pregnancy and delivery as normal. During the early teething stage, Gretchen developed a bad running ear condition. Together with this came a great timidness and shyness. Judging from the mother's report, there must have been a very serious intestinal trouble at the age of three and a half, with a surgical operation. After her recovery she had to learn many things over again—especially, had to be taught to walk. At four years she had chicken-pox; at six, whooping-cough; at eight, measles and mumps. At ten years she showed signs of goiter and was under a physician's care. It disappeared about a year after her menstrual periods began. Gretchen matured at the early age of eleven and a half. At fourteen, excessive menstruation started. Periods were too frequent and of too long duration. The physician treated Gretchen, but did not recommend an operation. He advised waiting for a year to give opportunity for adjustment.

Interpretation.—There is a poor physical history going back to the fourth year. The serious illness at that time could well account for timidity and lack of confidence at the beginning of her school career, which began as soon as she had learned to walk again. Although she had many childhood diseases, none of these caused a great deal of loss of time in school. Depletion of energy because of continued ill health must have been at least a contributory cause of poor learning. It is a certainty that during her first year of high school, ill health caused absence and a fatigue even when she was in school.

Although the goiter was reported to have disappeared, it was still palpable, and there was some slight evidence of nervousness. The physician reported that the goiter would bear watching, but it was not serious at this time.

Emotional History

During the most impressionable period of Gretchen's life, she saw nothing but sorrow, suffering, and agony. Her father was injured in an automobile accident and lingered for two years before he died. In this atmosphere of both mental and physical distress Gretchen's early adolescence was spent. There could not help being an emotional reaction from this type of family life spent amid gloom and suffering. Gretchen described the situation as "horrible." While the father was in the hospital the child sat at home and waited while the mother and son stayed with the father. The latter by nature was stern, and during his period of long suffering he was rather forbidding to Gretchen.

In an interview with the brother, he stated that his sister had always appeared very childish in her attitude toward everything, that she had thought him to be the favorite of the family and had looked upon herself as much inferior intellectually. During the last year he thought that she was growing up.

Interpretation.—Two factors are outstanding. First, the apparent preference of the family for the bright older brother, and his unusual scholastic record had kept Gretchen in a state of emotional upheaval and discouragement. The second factor is the serious accident which ended in her father's death. This, no doubt, added to the discouragement and feeling of not belonging, for we note that Gretchen was left behind during the visits to the hospital while the son accompanied the mother. Everything led Gretchen to close up, to keep everything pent up, and to feel a family outsider.

School History

Gretchen started her school career in a kindergarten of rather mediocre standing. She was about four and a half years old at the time. Up to this age she had been under the attentive care of a nurse in the home. At a very early age she felt a little jealous prejudice toward the first-grade children because they seemed to know so much, to be so important, and to be so sure of themselves. In kindergarten she used to sit back and marvel how the children could romp and scream and laugh so freely and not feel ashamed. At six she entered the first grade in a large public school. She always disliked school until fourth grade, when she liked the teacher very much and worked hard to succeed. Gretchen gave as her reason for disliking school the fact that she felt held down and couldn't play. According to Mrs. Kreutz's story, going to the first grade was like going into another world, as if she were breaking all home ties, for Gretchen had always been very strong in her likes and attachments and had been most devoted to her nurse.

The only fact outstanding in Gretchen's mind about her early school is that in the early part of the first semester of the third grade she injured her leg and was out of school for the rest of the year. When she returned the following September, she was promoted into the fourth grade without making up any work. Her arithmetic began to be hard then. From the time the class began to study the work involving fractions she never understood much about arithmetic.

A visit to the public school and interviews with the principal, the fourth- and fifth-grade teachers, brought to light very few facts. No records could be found, not even an attendance sheet. Her fourth-grade teacher remembered Gretchen very well. She stated that she was a plodding, not overly brilliant, but very conscientious child. She was always ambitious, associating with the best students in the room, and *ever striving* almost hopelessly to be at the top. She was timid and reserved, usually blushing violently whenever she recited.

Her fifth-grade teacher remembered her as an eager pupil who in the fifth grade was proud to stand eighth in rank in a class which the teacher characterized as a superior group for the public school.

When she was ready for 6 A, Gretchen entered another public school. Her first report card in this school is interesting in the light of the Will-Temperament test which seemed to indicate that Gretchen had little ability to adjust herself to a new situation. It seems advisable to quote the grades and to note the improvement. The four grades represent a semester's work.

English.......F, F, G, G *	Drawing........F, F, F, G
Reading.......G, G, E, E	Spelling.........E, E, E, E
Arithmetic.....P, F, G, E	Deportment.....E, E, E, E
History.......G, G, E, E	

Half days absent 3 0 0 2
Times tardy 0 0 0 0

* Explanation of marks: E = excellent; G = good; F = fair;
P = poor.

One should question the credibility of such a marked
improvement in arithmetic in 6 A. No doubt Gretchen
was marked on daily-lesson performance. She ended the
6 A, however, with an E in arithmetic. Yet in the seventh
grade it was well impressed on Gretchen's mind that she
almost failed in her arithmetic. The work in seventh-
grade arithmetic had to do with geometric ideas. When
one considers Gretchen's complete failure in space per-
ceptions as shown in the Army Beta test, one does not
wonder at her difficulty with geometry. Her recommendation from the public school to the high school was
as follows:

Scholarship Average.—She learns slowly.
Attitude.—Gretchen does not put forth much effort. She
lacks confidence and does not seem to know when she has
learned a thing.

During her freshman year, Gretchen studied English I,
Latin I, mathematics I, and general science.

In April it seemed advisable to have Gretchen drop
general science, since she was so far behind the class
because of absence that she could not catch up. From
January 11 to June 3, Gretchen had missed thirty-one
full days. This amounts to six school weeks.

In mathematics she was a problem case, showing weakness in arithmetical background and extreme carelessness

in computation. She failed all tests on first trial in every unit, and one or two reteachings were necessary before she passed the unit. Whenever her instructor gave her special instruction, she would say to him, "It is no use, Mr. ————, I'm just dumb." A tutor devoted about two hours each week to reteaching Gretchen on the various units.

In English her instructor reported that she was weak in her written work:

Mechanics—Weak in punctuation, form and minor details; lacking in consistency in usage. Construction—She uses "run-on" sentences; shows weakness in relation of pronoun and antecedent. Many sentences are confused in meaning due to confusion in thinking; others seem to be confused simply because the pupil lacks the essentials of writing. She always seems more conscious of the mechanics of what she is writing than of the thoughts she is trying to express. In other words, details which should have been mastered earlier in the school career occupy the center of attention and thought, and the ideas to be expressed naturally become of secondary importance.

In Latin Gretchen was placed in a special section of Latin IA during her second year, as we have seen.

Interpretation.—Gretchen apparently entered school, even as early as four and a half years, a bundle of inhibitions. In the kindergarten she wondered how the other children could laugh and scream in pure enjoyment. Yet she herself would have loved to play and to do as others did. She did not feel on an equal footing with her school mates. An added burden came when she skipped half the third grade and went on into the fourth without making up the fundamentals in reading and arithmetic, for a real intellectual gap was left. A lesson-learning attitude made her do well when she liked the teacher, but also kept her on a nervous strain to try to keep up at the top. Her fourth-grade teacher said that she always wanted to associate with the bright girls and to be in competition with them. The eighth-grade teacher's recommendation is an added bit of evidence along the lesson-learning line: "She does not seem to know when she has learned a thing." No, because her idea had been to satisfy the teacher, and, unless the teacher said that she was through, she did not know it. From every side of the school history there was evidence of lack of confidence, self-distrust, and self-depreciation.

In the first year of the high school there was an added difficulty because of many absences on account of illness.

DIAGNOSIS

The evidence as presented above points to the conclusion that the cause of Gretchen's trouble may be classified as learning complicated by an emotional disturbance in the form of lack of self-confidence, further complicated by an apathetic attitude toward school, a lesson-learning attitude toward book material, and a physical weakness.

Primary Causation.—Gretchen's condition is primarily due to an emotional disturbance existing from early childhood which exercises a strong inhibitory effect in the form of a feeling of "dumbness" or stupidity whenever school work is presented.

Secondary Causations.—These appear to be threefold: (a) apathy and lack of driving interest toward school work; (b) lesson-learning attitude toward the whole situation; and (c) meager intellectual background and specifically critical inability in the fundamentals of arithmetic.

Contributory Causations.—These are (*a*) physical and (*b*) emotional: (*a*) a lack of physical energy due to poor nutrition, an irregular menstrual history, and a bad physical history running back to the third year; and (*b*) a condition of emotional depression caused by the illness and death of the father.

Support of Diagnosis

Even before Gretchen entered school she had heard so much praise of the brother in school affairs that she felt an inferiority which was all-consuming. She even felt resentment. Her lack of confidence runs through the whole story. This inferiority presented itself whenever she started to do any school work which was difficult on the face of it. "I am dumb," was her first reaction. The conflict was always: "Am I inferior—am I superior?" From this emotion, which was strong and occupied the center of interest to such a great extent, grew apathy, and a lack of drive toward the task. She was defeated before she had tried. The whole school situation at the beginning was artificial. School was a different world— a world of striving and excelling. The brother had been put on a pedestal because he was smart and brainy. His success, his school life represented marks, standings, and high honors which she felt she could never attain. Gretchen was thrown into a strife situation immediately. She was always matching up with her brother. A furious over-compensation developed in the form of lesson-learning. The competitive struggle was established. Even in the kindergarten *in school* she could not enter into things and enjoy them with the others, but *out of school* she loved to play. Lessons had always been exercises one did to satisfy a person. The mother stated that she never had any liking for school nor did very well until she had a teacher whom she liked and for whom she would work. Mark that she worked for the teacher. Studies have not brought pleasure of themselves. They have brought an amount of praise or blame in proportion to the teacher's satisfaction. The favorable report card incident showed both a desire to prove to her family, and perhaps to herself, that she was competent, and a feeling on her part not of learning but of satisfying the teacher. In the eighth grade the testimony was that "she does not know when she has learned a thing." Quite right, she has no way in herself of telling that she had.

There are two factors—malnutrition and the menstrual history—which of themselves produce listlessness and lack of interest, and these helped to accentuate the disinterest toward school which Gretchen had built up.

Constantly contributing to this vicious emotional distress had been the depression caused by the father's illness and death and the greater opportunity and necessity to turn inward and to be apart from the family.

The intellectual gap in arithmetic probably had its beginning in the fourth grade, when Gretchen had skipped the last half of the third grade. "From that time on," Gretchen said, "I couldn't do arithmetic."

Why distribute this tangle of difficulties in a fifteen-year-old high school girl in this fashion? How do we know which is first and which is second, what is the main chain and what is contributory?

In the first place, the preliminary examination exhibits lack of confidence, inferiority feelings, as apparently the outstanding trait; and the pupil's whole relation to the school can be understood in terms of this emotional difficulty. We next turn back in the case history in an endeavor to find a time when this condition did not exist, for it might be that it began, as in other cases the same condition did begin, as the result of some school failure, a failure which might be still the hampering condition. But we find it existed from the preschool years, and we seem to find the reason which explains its origin. The child's attitude toward school from the beginning was a perverted one and resulted in learning perversions, notably the lesson-learning attitude, which not only prevented any genuine success in school but served as a constant stimulus tending to keep alive the original malady. And so we arrive in the field of the secondary, or derived causes, that field with which the teacher is familiar and which the teacher is predisposed to account for in terms of innate or constitutional defect. More often, in similar cases, what is here secondary is primary. In such cases, the pupil is ordinarily perfectly normal up to about third or fourth grade, when an essential failure and non-mastery promotion sets up the inferiority situation, which then goes on to further complicate matters in its own way. In some cases, the compensatory reactions then take the form of getting into mischief, in others that of lesson-learning or the perverse effort to build up forms of symptoms of what the pupil is not but wishes he were.

It is of first importance to segregate the primary difficulty, for otherwise treatment results only in apparent adjustment and a relapse follows.

The interpretation or diagnosis which is here set up is only a reasoned hypothesis, to be justified or disproved as treatment develops. But it is not guesswork. If treatment had failed to produce expected results, it would have been necessary to reconsider the data, perhaps to seek further data, and to formulate a new hypothesis.

TREATMENT

After the diagnosis of the case was made, a conference was held with Gretchen's mother. No mention was made, however, of Gretchen's being a case for investigation. Emphasis was laid on encouragement at all times and on no comparison of Gretchen's attainment with that of any one else, least of all with that of the brother. The mother was extremely intelligent about the situation and said that every effort was being made by all members of the family to do just that thing. The worker told her that any adverse criticism in the form of report cards was very distressing to Gretchen and for that reason no such reports would ever be sent home. There was the finest cooperation on the part of the home, and any inferiority that Gretchen might have felt at home before had no foundation later as far as the worker could discover.

Diet was discussed in detail with Gretchen and her mother. It was made clear to both that Gretchen was not taking enough food to generate normal energy. The worker insisted that Gretchen eat a hearty breakfast every morning, that she add more fresh fruit and vegetables to her diet, and that she drink more milk. This was carried out most conscientiously.

The average daily intake had been previously 1,075 calories. Within two weeks this had been increased to 1,910 calories. Although the intake was not yet quite up to standard (2,300-2,600), nevertheless it had been almost doubled. There was a slight increase in weight and less languor in her manner.

COMPARISON OF ACTUAL AND REQUIRED FOOD INTAKE ON
TWO CANVASSES

Food Element	Gretchen's Intake on First Canvass	Gretchen's Intake on Latest Canvass	Required Intake
Protein	38 grams	74 grams	66-75 grams
Calcium	.62 of day's need	1.00	1.00
Phosphorus	.43 of day's need	.99	1.00
Iron	6 milligrams	11 milligrams	15 milligrams
Vitamin A	+ + +	+ + +	+ + +
Vitamin B	+ +	+ + +	+ + +
Vitamin C	+	+ +	+ + +

Next, the results of the numerous tests which Gretchen had been taking were shown to her and explained. Weaknesses were pointed out and advice given for improvement. To cope with her limited vocabulary and background, more extensive reading of a higher type of literature was recommended. After a month some improvement in that direction was evident, for she read *The Mill on the Floss, Jane Eyre, Fanny and Herself, The Royal Road to Romance,* and *A Window in Thrums.* It was the first time that she had read books of any significance.

It was the aim of the examiner in showing Gretchen her results to prove to her that as far as mentality is concerned, she is not inferior but is on a par with the average student in her class. Her own scores and the comparison of these scores with the norms interested her and seemed to give her satisfaction. For some time after this she seemed happy and more self-confident. It was rather difficult to make her appreciate the difference between learning for a teacher and learning for learning's sake. The lesson-learning idea had become so ingrained that there was much doubt in the worker's mind whether the distinction was clear to the girl and whether she comprehended its full meaning.

At this time no remedial work was done along the lines of arithmetic because there were so many more pressing demands that it was thought best to do nothing about arithmetic because she was not taking any subject in which it is a much-needed tool.

A very definite attack was made on her health. Her attendance was very good until after the mid-year. During that interim she enjoyed a brief vacation and engaged so strenuously in the social festivities that her former trouble, dysmenorrhea, returned. From that time on her attendance was irregular. The worker got in touch with the home immediately, and Gretchen was taken to her family physician. The latter did not seem concerned with the situation, but gave her some treatment. He did suggest, however, to the mother that if the condition did not improve, it would be necessary to take her to the hospital for a complete examination. Both the home and the school watched the situation closely, and the home was eager to act on the suggestions of the school.

The fact that there had been old goiter trouble and that the thyroid gland was still palpable led to the giving of a metabolism test. According to the reading Gretchen's metabolism was normal and there was nothing to indicate thyroid disturbance. Furthermore, at the time of Gretchen's physical examination by her family physician he reported that he saw no evidence of hyperthyroidism.

It was encouraging to note that Gretchen began to make marked progress as soon as the worker began to give her personal attention. Each instructor sent in reports telling of the improvement in attack and also in the apparent growth in self-confidence. All encouraging reports were discussed with Gretchen and emphasis was laid on confidence, growth of independence, and the feeling of equality with the group. The case began to look exceedingly hopeful, and the semester reports were awaited with pleasure and eagerness by both Gretchen and the worker. In the latter part of January the old trouble, dysmenorrhea, started again and there was a poor attendance record for a short period.

Gretchen received the following reports for her first semester's work in the second year:

General Science.—Gretchen had some difficulty with the exercises, but by extra effort she has achieved a satisfactory result. In addition to the regular work she has reported a great deal of outside reading. She could improve her written work to some extent.

Latin I.—Gretchen has showed good attention and effort. Absence has interfered somewhat with her work. Her progress has been slow, but steady. Her increased interest, insight, and facility in any sort of dramatic material over that with narrative material is marked and interesting to note.

Ancient History.—Incomplete. Gretchen is handicapped as a student by absences, which she finds difficult to make up satisfactorily. She is well meaning and anxious to succeed, but is not strong as a student, and needs a good deal of attention. Her note work is just fair, and her expressions lacking in coherence. Her written papers show a difficulty in selecting and relating the large facts. She is very much in earnest and is improving.

English.—Gretchen has passed with some difficulty. She is very industrious and is very anxious to improve her work. At first her English expression was awkward and the organization was poor, but there has been constant improvement. She needs and deserves personal attention from the instructor.

The worker was pleased with the results. These reports all emphasized the improvement she had made, the effort and interest she was exerting, and the increase in attention. Ancient history was marked incomplete because of some tasks unfinished because of absence.

Within a week after the reports had been sent home, it was necessary to call Gretchen with some twenty other girls to the office to notify her that all subjects marked incomplete had to be brought up to date by the first of April.

The worker had had many conferences with Gretchen during her high-school course and she felt that she knew her very well, but she was wholly unprepared for the scene which followed. Gretchen burst into hysterical weeping as soon as she knew that her history was incomplete. This was the first evidence of tears which the worker had ever seen on Gretchen's part. The outburst on this occasion could not be quelled. For fifteen minutes no effort to quiet her brought results. The worker told her how satisfied she was with the report, how Gretchen was not the only one in the school who had received *incomplete,* how the whole report should be encouraging to her rather than discouraging, because each instructor mentioned improvement. At last Gretchen said, "Well, Miss ———, *I'm* not satisfied, *I'm* not encouraged. Now I know I'm dumb. I'm just cursed. Everything bad comes to me. If I have worked my *very,*

very best for four months and still get *incomplete,* I must be dumb. It is proof."

The same scene was repeated at home. Although the family praised her for all her other reports and said that they were proud of her, Gretchen saw nothing but *incomplete.*

From this time on the worker had an up-hill fight. The spirit had gone out of Gretchen. She was almost back to her original state of the fall—at least in history. Her absences increased, and at noon almost every day she complained of fatigue and sleepiness. Ancient history came in the early afternoon. One day she was truant and stayed out of school in more pleasant haunts. The worker realized that she was trying to get relief from a bad situation—a situation which had become unbearable to her.

To cope with the above, the worker made a complete change in her program. She was assigned to ancient history in the early morning. This was her most difficult subject, and it was hoped that she would be fresh for the attack at that hour. At the time at which she formerly had had history, she was sent to the girls' rest room and required to lie down and attempt to sleep. With the new arrangement most of her work (three classes) came in the morning. She had a noon period of relaxation and luncheon followed by a study period, then a rest period followed by general science, the last scheduled period of the day.

Matters began to mend almost immediately. Her history instructor reported that her attack on her work was better and her attendance had become more regular. Gretchen ended the year in good standing and with credit in all work. Her instructors made the following reports on the type of work she had done:

Science.—Gretchen's work in science is not brilliant, but it is entirely satisfactory. As far as time required to do the work is concerned and number of attempts she makes, Gretchen ranks in the lower quartile. Her attention and application in class are excellent. Her greatest strength is that she is trying to do the work in spite of difficulties which she has.

Ancient History.—Gretchen has completed all her work without having to rewrite a presentation or organization paper. There have been a few assimilative exercises which she has needed to revise. Her test scores show as rapid progress in learning as the average of her class. Gretchen has worked very hard. Her attitude is one of complete coöperation; her application is good. She has had some difficulty in comprehending the general story of an historical movement, seemingly because her background in history and her general vocabulary are a bit meager. She has ended the year in a creditable manner.

English.—Gretchen has made good use of her time in the class. When she began the course, her reading interests were narrow. She seemed to find difficulty in enjoying books which most pupils of her level find interesting. She has gradually come to read the more desirable books with pleasure. Gretchen at times has lacked persistence and when she has to undertake a difficult task she has a struggle with herself, but she has won in most cases this semester.

SUMMARY AND PROGNOSIS

At the close of this study Gretchen showed marked improvement. She was no longer the worried, nervous little girl who had hated to go to school and who had felt that all school was a competition. She was happy at school and at home, she was interested in school activities and liked her studies, she was a contented, conscientious worker. This relief from competitive strain was reported by the mother to be apparent in the home. Gretchen discussed her classroom work with the family and showed her interest in intellectual matters in many ways.

Her scholastic record showed improvement, too. She had passed all four of her courses in a creditable manner. It will be remembered that an "incomplete" in ancient history had caused such a great emotional upset in February that absence and truancy resulted. All this had been cleared up and Gretchen finished this course at the average level of her class.

FOLLOW UP

The change in Gretchen's spirit and the lack of emotional conflict made the result in the work of the junior year more commensurate with her natural ability. There was a marked gain in sustained application, there was definite growth in self-confidence and there was every evidence of improvement in methods of work. Reports of instructors at the end of the junior year follow:

History.—At first Gretchen was somewhat diffident and it seemed as if she could not enter into group discussion. There has been a noticeable change and improvement in this respect. Her work is above credit level. She has shown marked improvement in her capacity to express herself. Her whole attitude in the class has been commendable and I have enjoyed her as a member of my group.

English.—Gretchen is a steady worker with an excellent attitude. The quality of her work has improved throughout the year. She does not let any disturbance take her attention

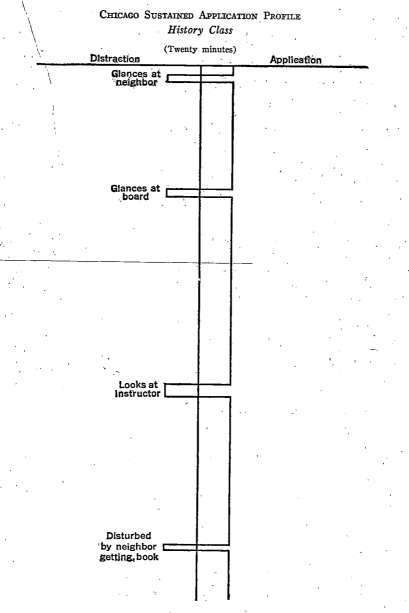

CHICAGO SUSTAINED APPLICATION PROFILE
History Class

(Twenty minutes)

Distraction   Application

Glances at neighbor

Glances at board

Looks at Instructor

Disturbed by neighbor getting book

from her work. As a consequence though not a brilliant student she steadily maintains a high level of achievement. She has quite mature tastes in reading and can express herself easily about books of adult level. Her writing shows a growing fluency.

Home Economics.—Gretchen's work has reached at the present time its highest level. At times during the semester she has given little thought to the course because, as she said, she was more interested in other subjects. She has, however, brought all work up to credit level in good fashion.

Music Theory.—Her attention is excellent and her achievement is of high order. Gretchen should plan to devote herself to the study of music.

Because of a change in the family finances, Mrs. Kreutz and Gretchen moved away from the city and her senior year was spent in an entirely new situation. Reports came from the other school that Gretchen graduated without difficulty. Since her graduation, she has devoted herself to the serious study of vocal and instrumental music.

CHAPTER III

THE SUPERIOR STUDENT: THE CASE OF
KATHERINE DUNCAN

KATHERINE DUNCAN, whose case is reported in this study, was a member of a sophomore class in high school. She was fourteen years and nine months of age. She was studying English III, Cæsar, Spanish II, ancient history, and geometry.

Katherine's case was studied that the worker might have a superior pupil as basis of comparison and contrast with the preceding problem case.

The worker chose Katherine as an example of a superior student because at the end of her first year in high school she was voted first place in scholarship by all members of the faculty in whose classes she was enrolled. She was characterized in the following manner: an interested, rapid, and accurate worker, prompt, efficient, exact, and independent, a student of unusual maturity.

INVESTIGATION OF PRESENT SCHOOL LIFE

Her work during the first semester of the second year had also been of superior quality. Her semester reports follow:

Study Hall.—Katherine has a real interest in things intellectual. With this interest she has a mental capacity for work which is rare for a pupil so young. She plans and organizes her work, concentrates fully, and utilizes every moment of her time to the best advantage. She takes full responsibility for her own work. We have had few pupils who have had the effective study habits which Katherine possesses.

Spanish.—Katherine is a wholesome, healthy girl of superior mental powers. She is doing two years of Spanish in one. She has a splendid linguistic background, having studied both French and German privately. She is alert, responsive, quick to see the point, and usually scores among the highest in tests. She has a good literary appreciation and excellent oral facility.

Geometry.—Katherine is a student with a keen mind, always willing to take the initiative. Her attitude in class is beyond reproach, and she works 100 per cent all of the time. Her work is neat and accurate and she always completes the assigned work. She can be depended upon to give the solution for a problem when the rest of the class has failed. While she is independent, and willing to take the initiative, she is of a quiet and retiring disposition. She has been excused from class routine several times. Her written and oral expression show understanding. She is able to think through a problem.

Latin II.—Katherine has the real reading adaptation. She is reading independently of the class and is doing a thorough and satisfactory piece of work. Although her grammar units are not perfect on the first test, she shows thorough comprehension of the principles involved. I commend Katherine for her work.

English III.—The most startling characteristic which I have noticed in Katherine's work is her immense reading background. I believe I am safe in saying that I have encountered no high-school student, regardless of age, who has shown evidence of so extensive a knowledge of general literature. I should add that this seems to be confined pretty largely to classics. I do not believe that she has read much, or so far is greatly interested in, contemporary literature. Another notable characteristic is her critical capacity. She not only reads widely, but she shows both an understanding and an appreciation of what she reads. There is nothing superficial in this aspect of her work. She is thorough, logical, original. I have rarely encountered among high-school students one who has so ready a vocabulary, and such an appreciation for the use of the right word. When called upon to participate in group activity, she produces the same good results, and I believe she is the guiding influence of her group. At any rate, every one respects her ability. On the other hand, I feel that she much prefers to work alone, choosing her own problems for study.

Katherine had shown unusual aptitude for foreign languages and English literature. She was, however, an outstanding student, showing a well-rounded development in all her work. She had well-defined habits of concentration and study.

Tests

Mental Tests.—This report contains three intelligence tests given to Katherine—the Terman Group Tests of Mental Ability, given at the age of 12 years, 11 months; Thurstone's Psychological examination, given at the age of 14 years, and Army Beta, given at the age of 14 years and 9 months:

Test	*Results*
Terman	I. Q. 144
	M. A., 18 years, 7 months
	C. A., 12 years, 11 months
Thurstone	134 attempts, 124 correct
Army Beta	104 correct out of a possible 118
	Grade A: very superior intelligence

The Terman test was taken at the age of 12 years and 11 months, and shows a mental age of 18 years and 7 months. In every phase of the test she showed marked maturity. Her general information, her vocabulary, and

ANALYSIS OF TERMAN GROUP TESTS OF MENTAL ABILITY

Test	Number Correct	Number Attempted
Information	19	19
Best Answer	10	11
Word Meaning	30	30
Logical Selection	17	20
Arithmetic	7	11
Sentence Meaning	23	24
Analogies	17	17
Mixed Sentences	17	18
Classification	13	18
Number Series	11	12

her interpretation of sentence meanings were most unusual.

Katherine's score in the Thurstone is 12 points above the third quartile of the senior record for the M—— High School. In no part of the test does she show any weakness.

RESULTS OF THURSTONE PSYCHOLOGICAL TEST

	Number Correct	Number Wrong	Number Attempted
Katherine's score	124	10	134
Sophomore			
Quartile 1	75.3	(75 per cent of class received this score or above)	
Median	88.1	(50 per cent of class received this or above)	
Quartile 3	101.3	(25 per cent of class received this or better)	
Senior			
Quartile 1	85.8		
Median	100.0		
Scale	112.4		

ANALYSIS OF THURSTONE PSYCHOLOGICAL TEST

Test	Number Correct	Number Attempted
Informational Questions	24	27
True-false	14	17
Identical Meanings	16	17
Completion of English Sentences....	16	17
Number Series	18	20
Relationship	35	36

The results on the Army Beta (non-language) Test corroborate the high I.Q. secured on the Terman and Thurstone tests.

Katherine did three of the seven tests perfectly and completed each of them in less than the allotted time. Perfect scores were secured on (1) the maze, (2) the series, (3) the fitting of geometric designs into a square.

Reading Tests.—Katherine scored as follows in the battery of reading tests given:

Test	Katherine's Score	Norm for Grade	Percentile Rank
Gray Oral Tests			
Rate	52 per cent	56 per cent	75
Quality	2 errors	5.9 errors	93
Thorndike-McCall Reading			
Scale	34	30.2	98
Van Wagenen Reading Scale			
Science	103	82.7	98
Literature	104+	82.1	98
History	92	85.4	95
Burgess Silent Reading Scale			
(Form I)	19 out of 20		

Arithmetic Tests.—The worker was very much interested in securing results on the Reavis-Breslich test, because the mother, when she had been asked on a school questionnaire, "Did Katherine ever have special difficulty in any school subject?" had answered, "Yes. She had trouble in arithmetic because she is very slow."

DETAILED RESULTS OF REAVIS-BRESLICH DIAGNOSTIC TESTS IN THE FUNDAMENTAL OPERATIONS OF ARITHMETIC AND IN PROBLEM SOLVING

Test	Number Attempted	Number Correct	Time Given, Minutes	Median, VIII A
Tests I—VIII				
Addition		9	3	
Subtraction		4	1.5	
Multiplication		5	3	
Division		3	4	
Addition and Subtraction of Fractions		9	2	
Multiplication and Division of Fractions		1	2	
Placing Decimal Point in Multiplication		10	.1	
Placing Decimal Point in Division		2	1.5	
Score: I—VIII		43		38.53
Test IX: Problems without Numbers	8	8	6	4.42
Test X: Problems with Numbers	9	9	4	8.16

In this test she is above the average in all three divisions. A weakness in multiplication and division of fractions is noteworthy. Apparently children of very superior intelligence ratings do not always master fractions.

Apperceptive Mass.—The following tests were given to Katherine with these results:

STENQUIST MECHANICAL APTITUDE TEST

Test	Katherine's Score	Median for Boys	Katherine's Percentile Rank
Test I	46	40	64
Test II	61	35	99.1

In the Inglis Tests of English Vocabulary Katherine made a score of 103, her percentile rank being 98 (median, 54.2):

	Possible Score	Attempts	Correct
Page 1	50	45	36
Page 2	50	46	38
Page 3	50	33	29

Katherine shows a wide range of vocabulary in all fields. The results on the Stenquist are most unusual. In both tests Katherine is above the norm for boys, but the result of the second test is startling. Her percentile rank is 99.1 on the scale for boys. During her freshman year in general science her instructor stated that in this elementary course Katherine had covered as much work as some people cover in a physics course. Apparently her general science carried over to this test.

Present Physical Record

Katherine's physical examination showed that she was 5.3 inches above the average height for her age and was 7.7 pounds over the weight for her age. Hearing, vision, and neuromuscular coördination were all normal. Diet was satisfactory. Teeth were in good condition. The tonsils were buried, but the doctor did not advise removal. The thyroid gland was palpable, but had caused no difficulty.

On her last physical examination she was marked *good* in general health. She did, however, show some slight evidence of nervousness, as she was in the habit of biting her nails and jumping at the slightest noise.

INVESTIGATION OF LIFE OUTSIDE OF SCHOOL

Family History

Katherine came from a line of Scotch ancestry on both sides. The paternal grandfather was a Highland sheep-farmer on one of the islands off the west coast of Scotland. He came down to Glasgow, married a Lowland woman, and set up in the wool trade. He was an odd mixture of sternness and sentimentality. English was an acquired language with him. He spoke Gaelic until he was nine years old. His English is said to have been beautiful and unmarred by colloquialisms.

The maternal grandfather was a native of one of the border towns in Scotland, and he married a woman who was a Highlander. In Scotland he became an architect and followed his trade when he moved to New York. He served in the Civil War at seventeen years of age.

Katherine's father is an excellent scholar and in his youth carried away many prizes, especially in Latin, Greek and French. Financial distress in the family made it necessary for him to stop school at the close of the high-school period. At nineteen he went to the Orient to work in his uncle's firm. He spent thirty years there, returning only after long intervals to Scotland. He now reads and speaks French and Spanish as well as his mother tongue.

Katherine's mother was born in the United States. Owing to misfortune she had but one year of high school. She is, however, well read, well informed, and shows real talent in music, art, and short-story writing.

A visit to the home revealed every evidence of a cultural background. Books, especially the classics in English, French, and Spanish, were in great abundance and were discussed as old friends.

Katherine is an omnivorous reader who prefers the classics. She has read and reread most of the works of Shakespeare and Dickens. She scorns magazines of almost every type and reads in them only when her parents suggest exceedingly worthwhile articles.

Health History

Katherine is the second of three children. The delivery was reported normal.

Katherine went through most of the childhood diseases before she was six years old. She had chicken-pox, influenza, measles, German measles, whooping-cough, and worms. None of these seems to have left any permanent effects.

Social History

The early years of Katherine's life were not spent among American playmates, as would have normally happened if she had lived in the United States. At fourteen she was old beyond her years and she had a well-developed imagination which had had plenty of time to grow during her lonesome days in a foreign land. It was the privilege of the worker to read Katherine's autobiography which she had recently written. A few excerpts from this will tell in expressive language what influences were working in the early years of her life.

She recalls the following incident which happened when she was four years old:

I liked to wander alone among the fields behind our house, and make up stories, full of the animals in Thornton Burgess's books. These constituted an "Army" of which I was the leader. As a matter of fact, everything that I did was developed by my mind in story form (a practice I still follow to a certain degree). I spent my time in elaborating on the imaginary adventures of the "Army." I did not like to talk of the Army to any one. One day when a little girl friend sat down in a chair which according to my conception was occupied by my right-hand lieutenant, Jerry Bear (he was more or less like Cæsar's Publius Crassus or Titus Valerius Labienus), I flew into a rage and dragged the astonished child away that she might not squeeze the breath out of him.

As one reads on in the autobiography, one is conscious of the vivid and lasting impression the early foreign life made on Katherine. To quote:

At certain times when I was five years old, we boarded the train for ———, a little village in the hills. After a long ride on the train, followed by a drive up steep, beautiful mountains in an automobile, we arrived in ——— just as the moon was rising. Beautiful sight! I can feel yet the wonder with which it inspired my childish soul.

A typhoon is coming. Then, the oyster-shell windows are closed, the doors made fast, lamps prepared against the departure of the electricity, and we, the house-mates, sit snugly in our wee room. I feel sheltered, safe and happy. I begin to love and appreciate the richness of home.

After her return to the United States, Katherine had been sent to a girls' camp during the summers so that she might become acquainted with American girls in sports and play. She enjoyed girls, but it was difficult for her to join in their chitter-chatter. She was mentally and intellectually beyond her classmates. This she regretted, for it gave her very few points of contact.

School History

Katherine lived in the Orient until she was six years old, and was under the care of a nursery governess from three years of age until she came to the United States. Her governess was a trained woman of intelligence, and Katherine learned to read, to spell, and to do some arithmetic before the age of six. The governess used the Froebelian methods.

During her first winter in the United States, Katherine lived in a small town in a north central state, amid the gloom of a household which waited for the death of a relative ill of an incurable disease. Katherine did not attend school in this town, but came in contact with three kindly spinsters who first introduced her to American literature. They read Hiawatha to her, and she says, "I loved it, but I did not understand it, yet I used to greet the sun every morning and pretend that I was East Wind talking to Hiawatha." She was equally fascinated by the tales from the classics told by the spinsters. She loved to sit by the hour and listen to *Romeo and Juliet,* and Mark Antony's speech after the death of Cæsar. A picture of Cæsar's murder so charmed her imagination that she was accustomed to take it up to an attic room, lock herself in, and gaze to her satisfaction at it.

Katherine's first school experience was a private school

in the East, where, her mother states, in the few short years she was there she developed personality, school spirit, and good citizenship.

At eleven she entered another private school in the East. At the end of her twelfth year in May she became a member of the school which she now attends. At that time she had an excellent speaking knowledge of German and carried the second year high-school French with excellence and ease.

During her freshman year she did work of outstanding character. Her reports follow:

Community Life.—A pupil who thinks across conventional lines and analyzes problems. She sees the superficialities and absurdities of many situations in civic life. A thinker who needs to be stimulated and encouraged. Satisfactory work throughout the course.

Latin I.—Katherine has done interested, independent, rapid, accurate work. She has done much work beyond class requirements, more difficult in quality, and has done it well.

General Science.—Katherine is outstandingly the best student in the class. She is prompt, efficient, and thorough in all of her work. She has led her class the whole year. She has almost a perfect score on all tests.

Algebra.—Katherine has made an excellent record in Math. I. She is a splendid worker, independent, exact, quiet, and commendable in every way.

English.—Katherine's reading maturity is considerably above the average for her group. Although she has not read extensively during the semester, she has read intensively and critically, always evaluating intelligently that which she reads. She has not confined herself to fiction, but has made herself acquainted with literature of various types. She read enthusiastically from Shakespeare and Chaucer.

A COMPARISON OF THE HISTORIES OF GRETCHEN KREUTZ AND KATHERINE DUNCAN

Family History

It is interesting to note that each of these girls in this study is of foreign ancestry, Gretchen descending from the Germans and Katherine from the Scotch. The paternal grandfathers in both cases were merchants. In actual schooling and degrees, Gretchen's parents are superior to Katherine's parents. In culture and intelligence apart from their academic credentials, the two sets of parents are perhaps on a parity. Both of Katherine's parents have toured the world and have come in contact with all types of people in various countries. They are adepts in French and Spanish. Their home life reflects the best in civilization.

School History and Social History

In this phase of the study, the contrast in the two cases is marked. Gretchen started to school at four and a half years; Katherine never was inside a school until she was between eight and nine. Competition was ingrained in Gretchen before she entered school; Katherine worked and learned at her own rate at home. Gretchen now learns a lesson; Katherine is seeking for knowledge. Gretchen cannot become absorbed in school work; on the other hand, intellectual matters are Katherine's all-absorbing interest.

Gretchen is immature in her reactions, she lacks confidence, and says, "I am dumb. Everybody knows more than I do." Katherine has confidence and maturity. This is shown in her autobiography. When writing about her tenth year, she says, "This year taught me much. It gave me a contempt for all weaklings, that is, the people who shirk life and fail to meet pain and work with a stiff backbone, who are everlastingly complaining of their hard lot which they themselves make hard, whose cowardice and foolishness tend to bring ruin on all around them." Katherine has learned a great lesson early. Her attitude toward life is purposeful and mature.

Katherine was reared among adults, having little contact with those of her own age, while Gretchen had normal play activities with groups of young children. Katherine's very early years were spent in extensive travel and in a most cosmopolitan atmosphere, from which she gained a broad and interesting background. Gretchen's acquaintances have been confined very generally to neighbors in an apartment-house district of a large city.

Katherine has read extensively and intensively in the finest literature written in English and French; Gretchen has found interest only in girls' stories and novels with fast-moving plots. Gretchen reads very rapidly, in fact, as rapidly as Katherine, but her energies have been spent on the trivial.

Physical History

Both girls have had many diseases peculiar to childhood and have been left with little after-effect. It is a coincidence that both at the age of ten to eleven were silent observers of adults who were suffering the tortures of disease. Gretchen came out of the experience shaken and nervously upset; Katherine came out with reserve and maturity.

Gretchen's course in high school has been interrupted by many absences. Katherine has had a good attendance record for two years.

Comparison of Tests

Physical Condition.—Gretchen is undersized and un-underweight, while Katherine is oversized and overweight. Neither girl has any defects in hearing, seeing or speaking.

Mental Tests.—The scores made by the two girls are reviewed for comparison in the following tables:

Test	Gretchen	Katherine
Terman .... Thurstone ...... Army Beta	I.Q. 94 78 attempts, 58 correct high average C +	I.Q. 144 134 attempts, 124 correct very superior A

ANALYSIS OF TERMAN GROUP TESTS OF MENTAL ABILITY

Test	Number Correct		Number Attempted	
	Gretchen	Katherine	Gretchen	Katherine
Information	10	19	17	19
Best Answers	8	10	8	11
Word Meaning	21	30	26	30
Logical Selection	13	17	16	20
Arithmetic	3	7	7	11
Sentence Meaning	13	23	19	24
Analogies	13	17	13	17
Mixed Sentences	11	17	12	18
Classification	13	13	15	18
Number Series	3	11	7	12

Gretchen was almost fifteen years old when she took this Terman, while Katherine was not quite thirteen. In this test Katherine shows her superiority over Gretchen in every type of question, but especially in general information, word meanings, arithmetic, mixed sentences, and number series. Katherine's *number correct* exceeds Gretchen's *attempts* in every case except one, Classification.

ANALYSIS OF THURSTONE PSYCHOLOGICAL TEST

Test	Number Correct		Number Attempted	
	Gretchen	Katherine	Gretchen	Katherine
Informational Questions	10	24	18	27
True-false	7	14	9	17
Identical Meanings	5	16	9	17
Completion of English Sentences	9	16	10	17
Number Series	10	18	11	20
Relationship	18	35	20	36

Katherine's score on each part of the test is almost double that of Gretchen. The greater difference between the two in this test as compared with the Terman Test is due to the fact that Katherine took the Thurstone one year and a half later than the Terman. No doubt the Terman results would be even higher if taken now. The number which Katherine has correct is far greater than the number of attempts made by Gretchen. This indicates that Katherine has both greater speed and greater accuracy.

In the Army Beta Test, Gretchen scored C and Katherine, A. Gretchen failed utterly on tests 2 and 7, both of which tested space perception. Katherine made almost perfect scores on these two sections in particular.

RESULTS OF READING TESTS

Test	Gretchen's Score	Katherine's Score	Norm for Grade
Gray Oral Test			
Rate	47 per cent	52 per cent	56 per cent
Quality	5 errors	2 errors	5.9 errors
Thorndike-McCall Reading			
Scale (Form F)	33	34	30.2
Van Wagenen Reading Scale			
Science	82	103	82.7
Literature	83	104+	82.0
History	81	92	85.0
Burgess Silent Reading Scale			
(P. S. I.)	12	19	

There is little difference between the two in the Gray Oral and the Thorndike-McCall. In the Van Wagenen test, Gretchen barely reached the norm for her grade, while Katherine was over twenty points above the norm on the science and literature tests, and seven points above on the history.

In the Burgess test Gretchen read twelve correctly out of twelve attempts; Katherine read nineteen correctly out of nineteen attempts. Here again the latter shows superiority in speed.

Katherine shows little superiority in the primary number adaptations, but is quite superior in the test consisting of problems without numbers. She made no errors in any of the problems and ranked far above the norm. In the intelligence tests which contained arithmetical sections, Katherine showed intelligence above average in handling this type of work, while Gretchen's scores were lowered considerably by weak work in arithmetic.

DETAILED RESULTS OF REAVIS-BRESLICH DIAGNOSTIC TESTS IN THE FUNDAMENTAL OPERATIONS OF ARITHMETIC AND IN PROBLEM SOLVING

Test	Number Correct		Time Given, Minutes	Median, VIII A
	Gretchen	Katherine		
Tests I—VIII				
Addition	2	9	3	
Subtraction	4	4	1.5	
Multiplication	5	5	3	
Division	3	3	4	
Addition and Subtraction of Fractions	1	9	2	
Multiplication and Division of Fractions	5	1	2	
Placing Decimal Point in Multiplication	8	10	1 .	
Placing Decimal Point in Division	8	2	1.5	
Score: I—VIII	36	43		38.53
Test IX: Problems without Numbers	1	8		4.42
Test X: Problems with Numbers	7	9		8.16

Two tests were given to determine apperceptive mass, the Stenquist Mechanical Aptitude Test and the Inglis Test of English Vocabulary. The scores made by the two girls in the Stenquist Mechanical Aptitude Test were:

Test	Gretchen's Score	Katherine's Score	Median for Boys
Test I	33	46	40
Test II	16	61	35

In the Inglis Test the compared scores are:

Page	Possible Score	Gretchen's Score	Katherine's Score
Page 1	50	21	36
Page 2	50	16	38
Page 3	50	13	29

The comparative scores on the tests given to judge apperceptive mass are most illuminative. Katherine doubles Gretchen's scores in vocabulary and far outclasses her in mechanical aptitude.

The Contrast

The predeterminist in education would probably dismiss the problem of the comparison between these two girls with the easy solution, one was born with a good mind and the other was not. How much do we know about it all? What do we know?

I. We observe that both girls came of stock which has shown itself to be adaptable and successful in its contests with the world. There are culture and intellectual life in both homes. So far as we know or can find out, there is nothing in either home to account for marked differences in success at school, save certain relationships between the siblings in Gretchen's case, as unnoticed by intelligent parents in her case as it probably would have been in Katherine's, had similar circumstances existed.

II. Gretchen had a trying physical babyhood, including a major surgical operation, the effects of which we know to have been sufficient to upset the learnings involved in walking. Katherine had the usual round of childish maladies, with no known lasting effects.

III. Everything in Katherine's early childhood was such as to launch her career in the confidence which is normal to childhood. Gretchen was handicapped from the start, not only by illness, which may have had organic consequences, but further by a sense that she was an "afterthought."

IV. In pre-adolescence and adolescence, Gretchen has existed on energy intake quite inadequate to normal growth and to the requirements of eager mental life. She has further experienced the drain of poorly established sex maturity. Both conditions were remediable. Katherine has been abundantly healthy throughout her early adolescence.

V. Katherine fell under the exclusive care of a trained teacher for her primary school years, who, judging from her profession, was concerned more with the pupil's development than with the formalized teaching of the school. At any rate, she had the exclusive attention of a trained person. Gretchen experienced the usual vicissitudes of a series of city public schools. If her teachers were adequately trained persons at all, they certainly did nothing whatever to analyze and correct the learning difficulties which the child was developing. They certainly had no conception of the consequences of the development of the lesson-learning perversion, especially in a child of Gretchen's unfortunate start.

VI. If the cases had been reversed in developmental history, Gretchen would not have been Katherine, nor yet Katherine Gretchen; but it is altogether likely that Gretchen's handicaps would have been handicaps to Katherine and the results similar, if not the same. Further, Gretchen's trouble has apparently been located and the girl has been given a belated start. It is hard to believe that it might not have been located early in her school career, with results, other things being equal, as notable as those which now appear to have taken place.

CHAPTER IV

PHYSICAL DISABILITY: THE CASE OF GEORGIA EWALD

GEORGIA EWALD, aged fourteen years, had transferred from a large public high school at the beginning of her sophomore year. She was enrolled in English II, history, Latin I and French II. At the mid-semester she was failing in two subjects and had reports of "incomplete" in the other two.

INVESTIGATION OF PRESENT SCHOOL LIFE

Instructors sent in the following diagnostic reports:

English.—Georgia is not doing creditable work in English II. The fundamental difficulty apparently has less to do with ability than with a sort of intellectual laxity. She seems to have no desire to expend the intellectual energy required to initiate any difficult reading. She appears nervous and fidgety and never seems really absorbed in any task. Her mind seems always to be on the outer rim of attention so that the slightest disturbance results in a break in concentration and application.

Latin.—Georgia's work has been ineffective and owing to frequent absences is incomplete. At times she has seemed to grasp the work very well, but at others she has exhibited diffused attention and has found it very difficult to concentrate on the task in hand.

French.—Georgia has not been doing satisfactory work in French II. First, she does not seem to have sufficient background to carry French at this level; second, she is absent so often that she misses much of the daily work; third, she is seldom able to stay after school to make up work as she is too tired. Her attitude is charming but her ability to stay with a piece of work until it is done is almost negligible.

History.—Georgia's written and oral work has been satisfactory both as to content and English usage. Absences are a handicap to her, however. She is behind the others and appears to be under a constant strain in trying to keep up her work. Her attitude is one of interest and coöperation. The nervous strain under which she seems to be working makes it difficult to urge her to complete her work.

Tests

Mental and Reading Tests.—The Otis Higher Examination gave Georgia an I.Q. of 109. She completed only 54 questions out of 75. She had 46 correct in the 54 answered. Her weaknesses were in number series and in "likes and unlikes."

In the Inglis vocabulary test, in which the class median is 65, she had a total of 55 correct answers.

Georgia's score for the Burgess Reading Scale was 44 (class median, 58.4).

The Thorndike-McCall test resulted in a score of 29 (median, 29.2).

In the Monroe Silent Reading Test (Rate) she received a rating of 109, the class median being 107.

Arithmetic Tests.—Georgia was also given the Reavis-Breslich tests, the results of which are shown in the table on page 89. Her score is 2.21 below the sixth-grade median.

A study of the arithmetic scores shows that with the exception of groups V (Addition and Subtraction of Fractions) and VIII (Placing Decimal Point in Division) the number of problems attempted by Georgia exceeds the

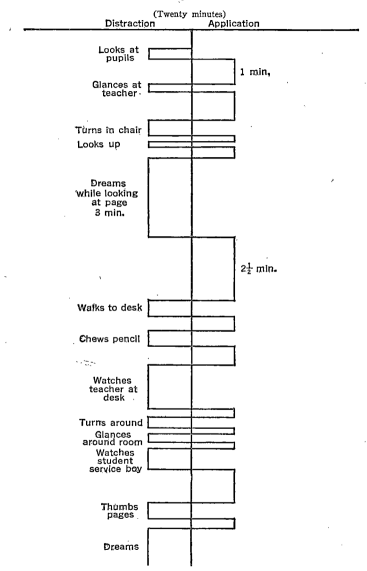

CHICAGO SUSTAINED APPLICATION PROFILE

Study Period

(Twenty minutes)

Distraction — Application

Looks at pupils

1 min,

Glances at teacher

Turns in chair

Looks up

Dreams while looking at page 3 min.

2½ min.

Walks to desk

Chews pencil

Watches teacher at desk

Turns around

Glances around room

Watches student service boy

Thumbs pages

Dreams

DETAILED RESULTS OF REAVIS-BRESLICH DIAGNOSTIC TESTS IN THE
FUNDAMENTAL OPERATIONS OF ARITHMETIC AND IN PROBLEM SOLVING

Test	Number Attempted	Number Correct	Georgia's Score	Median, IX A
Tests I—VIII				
Addition	5	4	4	4.02
Subtraction	8	6	3	5.42
Multiplication	2	1	1	4.37
Division	2	2	2	2.57
Addition and Subtraction of Fractions	6	2	2	4.62
Multiplication and Division of Fractions	5	3	3	6.26
Placing Decimal Point in Multiplication	11	9	5	8.78
Placing Decimal Point in Division	9	1	1	4.01
Test IX: Problems without Numbers	5	4	4	5.27
Test X: Problems with Numbers	8	6	6	9.91
TOTAL...................	61	38	31	53.75

number answered correctly by a small margin. On close
examination one is convinced that the total low score is
due not so much to lack of knowledge of how to do the
fundamentals as to a slowness in covering ground.

Georgia did not take any of these tests with ease. Restlessness and nervousness made her consume an unneces-
sarily long period of time in getting under way and there
was also evidence of tension throughout the whole testing
period. For this reason alone retests were not given.

Physical Condition

Georgia weighed fourteen and a half pounds less than
normal. Her eyes tested normal; her hearing was excellent. Her heart examination showed:

Pulse, normal 124
Pulse after exercise 150
Pulse after 2-minute rest 132
Loud systolic murmur at apex transmitted to
  left axilla and back.

The tonsils were found to be cryptic and hypertrophied; the cervical lymph nodes and thyroid gland palpable, though there is no noticeable enlargement of the neck. The basal metabolic rate is +30. Georgia has had many colds in the last three months and her nutrition is poor.

During the examination Georgia was restless, constantly tapping the table with her finger tips. She complained that she was thirsty most of the time and always drank from ten to twelve glasses of water a day.

SOCIAL RECORD IN SCHOOL

The fact that Georgia lived at a distance from the school made it necessary for her to leave for home almost immediately after dismissal of school and also kept her from any extensive participation in school activities of a social or extracurriculum character. During her short period of attendance she had made many friends and had been accepted cordially into the group. To all appearances she was happy and contented in her contacts with both girls and boys.

As the year progressed reports came to the worker concerning the exaggerated tales Georgia was circulating about her activities outside of school. At one time she told of giving an exhibition of a high-powered motor boat in a public park; at another time she boasted of entering an automobile speed race. All these exaggerations smacked of adventure and speed and were very incongruous considering her slowness of attack in school work and her usual modesty.

COMPOSITE PERSONALITY ESTIMATE OF FIVE TEACHERS

	High		Medium		Low	
Modest			x			Proud
Cheery		x				Peevish
Patient			x			Impatient
Courteous	x					Discourteous
Friendly	x					Reserved
Sociable	x					Unsociable
Imaginative	x					Prosaic
Altruistic			x			Selfish
Coöperative		x				Combative
Open-to-Suggestion		x				Opinionated
Contented		x				Dissatisfied
Optimistic		x				Pessimistic
Keenly alive				x		Apathetic
Loquacious	x					Taciturn
Self-poised						Flighty
Common-sense			x			Lacking in judgment
Frank			x			Underhanded
Honest			x			Dishonest
Reliable			x			Unreliable
Reasonable			x			Unreasonable
Prompt				x		Dilatory
Industrious					x	Idle
Attentive			x			Inattentive
Steady					x	Intermittent

Parents' Version of the Difficulty

Georgia's failure in school was as distressing to the parents as it was incomprehensible. Neither of them had any suggestions or solutions to offer. Report cards with excellent marks in every subject in every grade were produced as evidence of her scholastic achievement in former years and there was constant reiteration of the numerous advantages Georgia had always enjoyed. That their daughter should resort to prevarication was inconceivable and disgracing. They were inclined to feel that the school must have misunderstood the stories which were reported or that some one must have misquoted Georgia.

Pupil's Version

No coherent explanation could be gathered from Georgia. She had not intended to tell such wild tales. She just did not know why she did it. She felt fidgety and had had a bad cold so long that she was not herself. Every time she was absent because of illness she felt so far behind on her return that she scarcely knew where to start. She loved to do all sorts of things and she liked to go all the time. It was exciting to be "on the go." It worried her a great deal that she was not keeping up her work. She had always been an honor student and now look at the marks! She ran on and on giving no adequate expressions but emphasizing and corroborating the instructors' reports of restlessness and nervousness.

Interpretation

A consideration of the tests administered brings to light some important objective data. There does not seem to be incompetency as much as slowness in starting, restlessness and nervousness during the test. On investigation the Burgess and Inglis tests, as well as the Otis Intelligence Test, are low due to slowness rather than to lack of understanding of the material. In the intelligence test of seventy-five questions, Georgia missed only eight in the fifty-four which she attempted. The arithmetic test showed definite weakness in two types of work, the placing of the decimal point in division and the addition and subtraction of fractions. Obviously the educational tests do not give any reason for failure. One must seek further for the fundamental cause.

In the reports from Georgia's instructors only in French is there the suggestion that the pupil has not had adequate preparation for the work at sophomore level. All reports are filled with evidence of little concentration. Instructors say, "Her mind seems always to be on the outer rim of attention; her ability to keep her mind on her work seems very meager; she works under a constant strain; she exhibits diffused attention." One glance at the attention profile tells the same story. She has in twenty minutes only four periods of uninterrupted thought of one minute or more.

The physical report is most indicative as there is indeed serious evidence of physical disability. A palpable goiter together with an abnormally rapid heart, nervousness and loss of weight, cryptic and hytertrophied tonsils, poor nutrition, a slight temperature daily, constant colds, restless nights are factors which demand further investigation and immediate medical attention.

Georgia's exaggerated, adventurous story-telling may be sheer prevarication, a definite defense mechanism used in an effort to "put herself across," or it may be a compensatory gesture for her lack of success in the classroom or it may be the result of her serious physical condition.

INVESTIGATION OF LIFE OUTSIDE OF SCHOOL

Georgia had been born and reared in an apartment in a large city. She was an only child and her recreation had been usually with adults or with companions very much older than herself. Friends in speaking of Georgia's mother characterized her as "very literary" and a dramatic reader of uncommon ability. The father, a man of education and inherent refinement, held a position of responsibility in the business world. Both parents prided themselves on the type of books and magazines they read and had in the home. It was a well-known fact that Mr. Ewald refused to have or to read anything "trashy" as he called most of the popular magazines and books.

Because of reports of poor nutrition and loss of weight an extensive dietary study was made. The amount, the nourishing quality and the balance of food values were all satisfactory. It was obvious from this thorough investigation that reasons for the condition of underweight must be sought elsewhere.

Rest was inadequate in both character and length of period. Georgia reported that even on school nights she seldom had more than seven or seven and a half hours of sleep and usually she was restless, tossed about a great deal and dreamed very often. She was sleepy enough before she got into bed, but once she was there, sleep just didn't seem to come.

Until the present year she had been very active in sports and had been normally proficient in golf, basketball, baseball, tennis and swimming. Because of colds and some fatigue the recommendation of the school physician that she take no strenuous exercise and do little walking had been followed carefully. Therefore, she was entering little into physical activity of any kind, either in or out of school.

Social activities were numerous—in fact, too numerous. Concerts, opera, the theater, teas with adults, trips to museums and art galleries filled her time. In addition to her classes in school she took private lessons in conversational French, piano, violin and voice.

It was a source of gratification to the parents that their daughter had no interest in boys, "dating" and parties.

Interpretation

In this home of refinement, culture and intelligence the utter ignorance shown in the parents' conception of a normal, intellectual and social load for an adolescent girl is amazing. Under the misnomer "advantages," they have gone to absurd lengths in providing private lessons in cultural subjects and have robbed the pupil of sufficient rest. In no phase of Georgia's life is relief from tension or an opportunity for joyous, unadulterated play provided. Cut off from active sports because of fatigue and its partner, colds, she is plunged into a round of adult social activity, in many respects far more fatiguing than a gymnasium class. Furthermore, the parents state with pride that Georgia is not attracted to boys, that she does not go to girl-and-boy parties, that she reads only the classics. Yet these very activities which are not countenanced may be the very type needed by Georgia to provide a necessary let-down, to induce sleep, and to open up an outlet to an adventurous spirit. There is much in Georgia's life outside of school to account for nervousness and fatigue with resulting colds, malnutrition and rapid heart.

Physical History

The father was twenty-six years old and the mother twenty-four at the birth of Georgia. Pregnancy was full nine months. Delivery was by forceps. Weight at birth was seven pounds. Baby was breast and bottle fed and was reported to have made normal increase in growth. She walked at thirteen months and talked at about the same age. At four years she had whooping-cough; at six years she was vaccinated against smallpox; at seven years she had chicken-pox. All these diseases were mild in form and left no after affects of a serious nature.

Emotional History

The mother's own quotation best describes her early years: "Georgia has been reared well, having had everything she needs and demands but she has not become selfish, conceited, arbitrary or in any wise spoiled. She has always been happy and very busy. Her mind has always been joyous and pure."

School History

Aware of the absurd number of private lessons given to Georgia during her sophomore year in high school, the investigator was not at all surprised to discover that Georgia had been tutored by her mother before she entered the first grade and that during most of the elementary school years there had been tutors or governesses in the home. According to the teachers during this period there was no need at any time for additional assistance or instruction. All the extra work was given with the idea of providing additional advantages. Georgia had always stood at the head of her class in the grades. There had been no tutoring during the eighth grade or the freshman year in high school.

Report card for the last semester of the freshman year follows:

				Final
English literature	E*	E	E	E
General science	E	G	E	E
Mathematics	G	E	G	E
Social studies	E	E	E	S
French	E	S +	S +	S
Art	E	S	S	S
Music	E	G	E	S
Cooking	G	G	G	G
Physical education	G	G	G	G
Study efficiency	G	E	E	E
Social efficiency	E	E	E	E

* Marking scheme: *S,* superior; *E,* excellent; *G,* good.

The following recommendation accompanied the report card: "Georgia Ewald is one of our most delightful girls. I know her well inside and outside of school. She is an independent worker, her scholarship is excellent, her attitude most helpful and her personality charming. She will be a credit to your school both socially and scholastically."

Early history reveals no reason for complete breakdown in scholarship. There is, to be sure, a history of tutoring but the tutoring has been an added luxury rather than a necessity. Teachers of the first year of high school emphasize the independence of the pupil, and the excellence of her scholarship. Her report card shows excellency in study efficiency. French, a subject failed in the second year, was carried with honor the previous school year. Work in mathematics, too, was of high quality. The whole estimate of this student is diametrically opposed to the reports of her present teachers.

DIAGNOSIS

Primary Causation.—This is a physical case. A serious physical condition exists which is so powerful in its inhibitory action that the student is deprived of the ability to carry on mental work at her usual level of efficiency.

Contributory Causation.—The overstimulation and fatigue resulting from strenuous social life combined with an excessive number of private lessons aggravates the physical disability.

Support of Diagnosis

The thyroid is palpable. This fact would not be so serious were it not for the additional knowledge that it is persistently so and is combined with many other evidences of disease. Practically 75 per cent of girls in many cities in the Middle West at certain periods have palpable goiter.[1] The rapid heart, the loss of weight when the diet is adequate, extreme thirst, a basal metabolic rate of $+30$, and nervousness are symptoms which point clearly to the fact that the body is literally burning up tissue at too rapid a rate. The medical specialist's report

[1] Anold S. Jackson, M.D., *Goiter and Other Diseases of the Thyroid Gland* (Paul B. Hoeber, Inc., 1926), p. 60.

which verified and named the disease follows: "Thyrotoxicosis, *i.e.*, exophthalmic goiter. The predisposing factors are the infected tonsils. The secondary damage done is mitral insufficiency and malnutrition." Instructors in school reported Georgia as nervous, fidgety, never really absorbed in any task. The attention profile pictured her restlessness and the shifting of attention quickly from one thing to another. Every statement in the school reports, the physical report of the school physician and Georgia's account of her difficulty in resting all fit in perfectly with the description of a typical case of exophthalmic goiter as described by Bram:[2]

The patient though formerly capable of sustained physical and mental effort, is now quite different. The individual tires of the matter in hand more easily. He is enthusiastic, intense and eager for brief periods only. The marked lack of perseverance, shiftlessness, a tendency to hop from relevant to irrelevant thoughts, expressions and actions characterize the day's event. Excitability, restlessness, agitation, and sometimes depression are soon common attributes of thought and action. When evening comes, sleep is not a cheerful prospect, and when the patient retires attempts at rest are unsuccessful. The patient, though glad to leave bed, arises in the morning feeling tired and weary.

In many cases of exophthalmic goiter not only are there marked physical changes as have been noted but also mental changes which no doubt definitely account for Georgia's wild adventurous tales of speed. Bram states:

Mental changes varying from a mere inconspicuous change in temperament and disposition to an actual grave major psychosis are commonly seen in the disease. Occasionally, rest-

[2] Israel Bram, M.D., *Goiter: Non-surgical Types and Treatment* (The Macmillan Co., 1924), p. 167.

lessness, impatience and emotional outbursts may precede by weeks and months any definite evidence of the disease.[3]

Georgia, suffering from this serious disease of which the parents were entirely unaware, was not only permitted but urged to indulge in a round of social engagements which would exhaust an adult in good health. So the home life of this pupil has been an added aggravation to the disease.

The school has been asking the impossible from Georgia. In the light of the findings it is very doubtful whether the scores on the tests are at all indicative of Georgia's ability.

TREATMENT

On recommendation of the physician all outside activities were stopped, one subject was dropped and a rest period at the twelve-thirty hour was substituted. Milk was served to Georgia at ten and one o'clock. It was hoped that the relief of tension and the lessening of strain provided by more rest would improve Georgia's condition so that an operation would not be necessary.

Rest plays an important part in the treatment of goiter. Bram states:

By the term rest in the management of goiter is meant that state of body and mind wherein catabolic and degenerative processes are reduced to a minimum and anabolic and regenerative processes are enhanced. Rest aims at a reduction and elimination of that consuming overalertness or quickening of mental and physical processes characterizing the disease. To quiet and stabilize the circulatory tree, to overcome the excitability of the gastro-intestinal, genito-urinary, cutaneous and

---

[3] *Ibid.,* p. 165.

CHICAGO SUSTAINED APPLICATION PROFILE
Study Period
(Forty minutes)

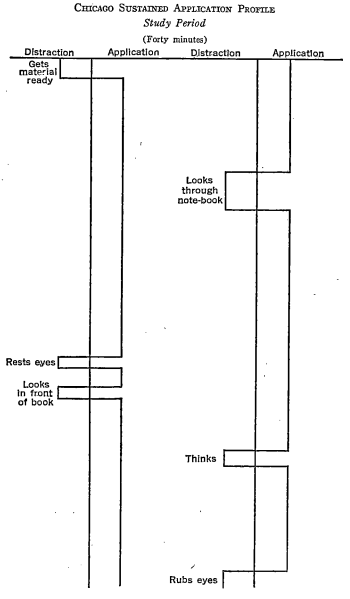

other systems of the body, to reduce the oxidation of the tissues and enhance the restoration of bodily weight and strength, and finally, to tranquillize the turbulent emotional status of the individual—this is the function of rest as a constituent of a broad management of Graves' disease.[4]

It was not long, however, before the physician recognized that the program was not proving satisfactory so he requested that Georgia be in bed for at least one month to provide complete relaxation preparatory to the removal of the goiter.

The program was followed, the operation was performed and Georgia was out of school for a six months' period. After her return to school her list of studies was French, art, English and mathematics. All instructors found her steady, deliberate and painstaking. Her reports follow:

French.—Georgia is a very satisfactory student, doing her work easily and well. Her attitude is fine in every way.

Mathematics.—Georgia is a hard worker. She attains credit level without any reteachings and without any difficulty.

Art.—Georgia is a very conscientious worker, applying herself diligently all the time. Her standards are very high and her work very creditable in every respect.

English.—Georgia has read widely throughout the year, and has responded actively to all discussions and suggestions. At times her comments in written and oral discussion showed remarkable penetration and appreciation of her reading.

No unfavorable reports were received in the four years she spent in the high school.

After graduation she entered a large state university where she has had a good record in the department of journalism.

---

[4] *Ibid.*, p. 296.

CHAPTER V

EXHIBITIONISM: THE CASE OF CLARA ROMBI

WHEN Clara Rombi entered the freshman class she was in appearance a pleasing, attractive and bright girl of fourteen. Her graciousness of manner and her *savoir-faire* were such that she would stand out in any group of adolescents.

Scarcely had the first month passed when almost simultaneously reports of failures in Latin, mathematics and science came into the office. In conference, Clara could always explain away her difficulties and her failures. At the very time that she began to fail in classes the habit of prevarication became evident. Instructors would report that Clara's work was incomplete. Clara would graciously explain that there must be some error, in fact, the instructor must have sent in the report before he realized that all her work had been handed in and had been checked. She knew that everything had been O.K.'d that very day. It became necessary to check up carefully on every statement Clara made. Both the instructor and Clara had to be present whenever a report of incomplete work was made to the office. Then and only then would she admit that she had not completed the work in a satisfactory manner.

INVESTIGATION OF PRESENT SCHOOL LIFE

Clara's teachers reported as follows:

Latin.—Clara's attention and effort have been intermittent and poor. Because of this she has failed utterly to get an adequate foundation. She is making a great effort now but it is impossible to make up for the loss of the early work and continue with the present work.

Science.—Clara has required a very large amount of reteaching and retesting. Papers are corrected and rewritten without any real improvement. Test scores, too, show very slow improvement upon repetition. Clara shows little understanding of the following units: Unit II, Weather and Climate, and Unit III, Foods. She is below the attainment of the class.

Mathematics.—Clara has not mastered the essentials even though she has had a great deal of time and attention from the instructor for reteachings. She finds it difficult to follow any systematic plan of procedure and tends to work by intuition. She is seldom able to find errors in exercises returned for correction.

English Usage.—Clara is reaching credit level but she is a very superficial learner. She is very dependent upon the instructor and does nothing unless she is absolutely required to do it. After much insistence and pressure she will attempt to use the knowledge gained in her work and apply it to her own written work. In spite of a decided nervousness in class, she is very guarded in her actions. I am wondering what she would be like and what she would do if she were off her guard.

Clothing.—Clara has been restive and has not developed good habits of study nor fine qualities of class citizenship. By repeated reteachings she has gained an understanding of the essential elements of the course.

Tests

In the Otis Higher Examination Clara attempted 72 items and answered 42 of them correctly. Her I.Q. is

109. Analysis of her test sheet reveals no particular type of difficulty. Her work was comparatively accurate on the easier questions. Her inaccuracies occurred on the more difficult questions in the test.

Clara attempted 102 questions of the Thurstone Psychological Examination and answered 79 of them correctly. The class median was 76.

In the Inglis Vocabulary Test Clara's score was 84. The class median was 66. Her percentile rank is .80.

Clara marked correctly 26 out of 31 paragraphs in the Chapman Test of Reading (Comprehension). The class median was 22.1. Her percentile rank is .87.

In the Monroe Silent Reading Test she made a *comprehension* score of 48. The class median is 36. Her percentile rank is .84. She attempted every paragraph in the test but marked three of them incorrectly. She made the highest *rate* score possible on this test. Her percentile rank is therefore 1.00. Her score is 151. The median for her grade is 107.3.

Present Physical Condition

Clara's general physical condition was excellent. Her sight, when she was wearing glasses, was excellent. Her hearing was good, and her pulse 78. She showed signs of nervousness, however, during the examination. She was restless, fidgety and extremely loquacious.

Social Record in School

At the beginning of the school year Clara had been accepted into her class group without question. In fact, girls had liked her so well, at the beginning, that they had elected her to a minor office in the Girls' Club. Stu-

dent approval did not last long, however. Soon girls
from every grade level complained that Clara was constantly criticizing them, that she was unbearable, dictatorial and sarcastic, that she was overbearing and wanted
to dominate any group in which she chanced to be.
Although obvious unpopularity was now Clara's lot she
continued the same irritating conduct with her classmates.
Therefore, the year was barely under way when Clara
became the class joke. The girls liked to see her perform so they began to frame situations in which Clara
would be the proverbial "goat." Conscious or unconscious of their gibes Clara seemed to enjoy holding the
center of the stage even though bought at the price of
ridicule.

The following characteristics were used to describe
Clara by both faculty members and her mother: fussy,
nervous, quite impervious to criticism, resentful, opinionated, lacking in judgment, self-poised, optimistic, refined,
courteous, cordial, sociable, vain, dilatory, inattentive,
intermittent, unreliable and loquacious.

Mother's Version of the Difficulty

Mrs. Rombi was most coöperative in trying to help to
find a solution of Clara's problem. She admitted that her
daughter told her only what she was forced to explain.
There was always evasion of actual information unless
a regular upheaval took place in the house. As far as
Clara's having any real difficulty with learning Mrs.
Rombi felt that it was impossible, for her school work
had been completed heretofore with ease. Surely there
could not be such complete collapse in learning within so
brief a period! Inasmuch as Clara had few social en-

gagements except an occasional simple afternoon party and the movies and considering the fact that Clara had received no attention from boys her time and attention were not occupied outside of school. With the most sincere desire to help she said, "I shall consider it a favor if you will show Clara no leniency. Make her come to terms. Show her no mercy. Please insist that she do everything up to the minute. Tell her that if she is behind in as little as a single exercise that you will notify not me but her father. I think that you will get action then!"

Clara's Version

When Clara was encouraged and urged to talk freely about her failures in school she assumed a rather sophisticated pose. Oh, yes, she knew that her thinking was very disorganized, but she believed that it was due entirely to lack of sleep. Her evening dates were so numerous and lasted so late that her hours of sleep were very limited. A person of her habits should expect stupidity at eight o'clock in the morning because her sleeping quarters were thick with smoke, caused by the excessive indulgence in cigarettes by herself and her girl friend with whom she spent many, many nights.

Following the suggestion of Mrs. Rombi, during the conference, it was announced to Clara that the next unfavorable report in any subject would be sent to her father at his office, not to her mother. Immediately there was a definite change in attitude. Her eyes opened widely, and she breathed fast and loudly, and she pleaded, "Oh, don't. Please, don't do it." In almost a desperate manner she muttered half aloud: "How can I work when

I get here? I awake in the morning feeling perfectly great. If I get up at seven my father complains that it is too early. On the other hand, if I wait until seven-ten or -fifteen, he says that it is too late. I can't satisfy him. Out of a clear sky he flies off the handle about nothing. Then, mother and I catch it. I have to have a chance somewhere, don't I? I have to live, you know. I live here at school. Don't tell him about anything here, please!"

Interpretation

All indications are that Clara is both a learning and a conduct case. She is failing in most of her classes. Yet there is evidence of good mentality. Clara's performance on tests shows her to be capable of doing work equal or superior to the members of her group. On tests of vocabulary, comprehension of reading, rate of reading and arithmetic she ranks in the upper quartile. In addition to failure in scholastic work she shows behavior difficulties. She is resistive and impervious to criticism; her attention is spasmodic; she prevaricates to her instructors, to her mother and to her companions. Compensation is apparent in her dictatorial, overbearing attitude toward her fellows, her stories of wild, long-protracted parties, excessive cigarette smoking and the discrepancy between her own stories of life outside of school and the account given by her mother. There is evidence of definite friction between the girl and her father.

INVESTIGATION OF LIFE OUTSIDE OF SCHOOL

Mrs. Rombi worked part of each day, but she had never permitted her business venture to interfere with regularity of meals and the careful consideration of a well-balanced diet for Clara. Trained as a home economics teacher, she had carried over into her home life household efficiency. Although the home was average in many respects, it showed intelligent management, good taste and good housekeeping.

Clara was an only child, and she had been given good care from babyhood. Social affairs during the school week were unknown in the home. Clara was in bed and asleep before nine-thirty on school nights. Her week ends were quite simple and rather uneventful.

One could not be a visitor in the home for even a short period of time without feeling a strain and tension all the time. Mr. Rombi was quiet, courteous but gruff. Mrs. Rombi talked fast in a high-pitched tone. One felt that she hesitated to stop lest something happen. Clara spoke very little and during most of her conversation she cast furtive glances at her father to see if her remarks met with his approval.

Mrs. Rombi reported that from the child's birth her father had been extremely jealous of the intimacy between the mother and child. He always showed extreme emotion toward Clara. At times he indulged her with every extravagance, again he refused to give her the bare necessities. Now he was affectionate, calling her by endearing names while in almost the same breath he punished and maligned her, saying that she was a thief and a liar and he would have nothing to do with her. When speaking to Mrs. Rombi about Clara he always referred to her as "your child." During the absence of Clara from home the household was calm, pleasant and peaceful. The very mention of her return raised a storm of quarreling, disagreement and open hostility.

Interpretation

The picture of the home corroborates the evidence given before of friction between Clara and her father. The intensity of this friction is ominous for natural development of any child.

EARLY HISTORY AND DEVELOPMENT

A study of the histories of both mother and father showed nervous instability on both sides. On Mr. Rombi's side there was mention of nervous indigestion and serious nervous breakdowns in the lives of the paternal grandfather and uncle. The maternal grandmother was irritable, nervous and queer.

Physical History

Clara's birth was normal and at full term. She was a breast-fed child. Talking and walking were reported at a date which would make her exceedingly precocious.

As a small baby she was nervous, slept lightly, cried a good deal and was very fussy. Her early history was singularly free from diseases of childhood. At nine, Clara had serious swollen glands and underwent a mastoid operation. Her recovery was complete and satisfactory in every way. Since that time, Clara had been a very healthy little girl.

Emotional History

Mrs. Rombi had been married while very young to a man thirty years her senior. Their early married life had been happy and complacent but there was a decided change in the home when Mrs. Rombi announced her pregnancy to her husband. His attitude was one of jealousy, disgust and irritation. He declared that he didn't want the baby, that his wife was all the baby he needed and he vowed that he would have nothing to do with any child after it was born.

Since there was lack of sympathy and constant disharmony during the period of pregnancy, it is not surprising that Clara was a nervous, irritable and fussy child for several months after her birth. As a result of this irritability, Mrs. Rombi was kept nervously on edge and in a state of fear lest the newborn baby disturb her husband to such a degree that he would leave her and seek the quiet and peace of another home. So, very early in life Clara had been taught to be tactful and diplomatic far beyond her years. From babyhood she had been led consciously and unconsciously to evade every issue with her father, and to keep from him everything which might cause a scene for herself or her mother. Therefore, it is to be expected that, at thirteen, it was second nature to Clara to paint the picture just a bit different and never actually to face the truth.

School History

From kindergarten to high school Clara's education had been secured in an excellent public school in a large city. She had attended but two different schools in eight years.   Learning had never been difficult for her although she had never excelled in that type of work. · Her elementary-school teachers all stated that she had done well but they doubted that she was living up to her capacity.   Early in the grades she had displayed charm of manner and a capacity for lying in matters of little importance.   Teachers had found her agreeable, likable and no scholastic problem.

DIAGNOSIS

Primary Causation.—The fundamental difficulty is a deep-seated feeling of insecurity.

Secondary Causation.—Compensatory behavior is shown in an urgent and insistent drive to establish herself.

Tertiary Causation.—The result is (*a*)· a lack of interest in school work and (*b*) prevarication.

Contributory Causations.—These are (*a*) an inherent nervous instability which makes Clara more susceptible to emotional upset, and (*b*) constant friction in the home between the mother and the father, and the father and Clara.

Support of Diagnosis

All evidence in the case shows that there is nothing in the intellectual background which would account for poor and failing work in school.   Lack of learning must come as a result of other matters.   In every learning product we know that there is a volitional as well as an intellectual component.   At the root of volitional retardation there is usually an emotional perversion which causes the lack of · attack.   Clara felt insecure.   As far back as her first knowing moments she knew that she could not please her father. From one action at one time she got the response of enthusiastic approval on the part of the father. The very same action at another time would bring sarcasm, rebuff and even severe punishment. The world in which she lived was uncertain, unsteady. What part had she in it?

Clara had felt from the beginning that she was not wanted at home. As long as she was young, and even in the pre-adolescent period, she had taken the attitude for granted and probably had never questioned why she was not wanted. As she began her high-school course she entered the adolescent stage, and adolescents by nature seek explanations and compensate. At home she was a nobody and didn't amount to much. Didn't her father call her "liar" and "thief" and prophesy that she would never amount to anything? Wasn't she called her mother's child? Did she really belong to the father? Seeking, seeking for some explanation and trying to gain a security of feeling naturally led her to behavior difficulties. Reality was harsh so she began to make an unreal world which was much more satisfying. In her world of daydream she was very important. She was the center of attention. She went out constantly with young men, was popular and enjoyed parties and "high life." She smoked and kept late hours. Everything, in fact, was in sharp contrast to the distasteful humdrum existence of her real life. In school companionships she must put herself across. In her home she had no peace nor any authority, so in the school she was domineering, impervious to criticism and omniscient. As she expressed it, she "lived." The hand of authority in the home did not reach into the school. It was only when the school suggested that reports of failure were to be sent to the father that the hand of home authority was present, and the real Clara saw her dream world evaporate, and she cried pleadingly, "Oh, don't! Please, don't!" Insecurity had crashed again into the situation. In the struggle to put herself across and to gain for herself a feeling of self-confidence and secure position, her attention was so completely absorbed that there could be little left over for school tasks. She did only as little as she was compelled to do in order to be let alone so that she could live in her unreality. So potent was this unreality at times that even to herself prevarication was not prevarication. She refused to recognize reality, and in the case of science said that tasks were completed and O.K.'d when they were not. Again, in her effort to put herself across it is interesting to note the growth of the prevarication and the lengths to which she would go. At first, she merely showed unusual leadership, so called, so that she was given a place of prominence in the girls' organization. This for a time made her feel very secure. Soon she realized that in this position she was really not very great, and she thirsted for power. The next step was domineering bossiness and obnoxious egotism. Realizing that she was failing she fought for the comfortableness of security and made up stories which she believed would give her a conspicuous place with her comrades. Inasmuch as she lived a quiet, protected life and most of her comrades did the same, the life which she pictured to her friends was one of freedom, unrestraint and dare-deviltry. What a person her friends would think her to be!

A strong contributory factor is the inherent emotional

weakness. The families on both sides showed nervous instability. On the father's side there had been serious nervous maladies in both the paternal grandfather and the uncle. The maternal grandmother was known to be "queer." There is no doubt from the evidence in the history that Mr. Rombi could not have been well balanced. With such a family background of instability there was plenty of reason for emotional upset in Clara. Add to the family history the distressing and serious conditions of the pregnancy and one has a most fruitful field for emotional turmoil. An ever-present and powerful irritant was the constant friction at home. There was little time each day that Clara was not subjected to the insane whims of the jealous, selfish father. Therefore, each day as Clara set out to gain security and comfortableness she met defeat. Thus the problem became constantly more complicated and unsolved. The result was failure in school and that, too, brought greater insecurity and called for greater compensation. Clara, the victim, was the vortex of the whirlpool and so her escape had to take the form of a world of unreality where she made things come true and in which she was comfortable and safe.

TREATMENT

No permanent cure could be gained until both the parents especially the father recognized the underlying cause of the difficulty. The father had to realize the seriousness of his hateful attitude. Furthermore, unless Clara herself could be made to feel that she was wanted by both mother and father and unless the tension in the home was relieved, the feeling of insecurity and inferiority would still be there and Clara would continue to compensate.

To reach the father was the most difficult task as he never came to the school and all the discussion with him of Clara's difficulty had to go through the mother. Naturally there was emotional coloring in her interpretation of our statements. Little progress was made with the father who had long ago passed the age of ready adaptability and who apparently had never liked children.

As simple an explanation as possible was made to Clara. An attempt was made to make her understand that daydreaming was futile for permanent adjustment. Emphasis was laid on compensating in the form of something concrete and tangible, such as good class work and good social attitudes. Sympathetic help was assured through the instructors who were informed of the exact difficulties in the problem. For one so young Clara seemed to have rather unusual insight into her case. During the rest of her freshman year she seemed to try very hard. It was too late for Clara to make up her work in Latin. In the other subjects with much additional instruction and a great deal of extra help in after-school periods, Clara completed the required work and received credit in her courses in science, mathematics, English and clothing.

During the following summer Clara was out of the home from the day school closed until a few days before it opened again in the fall. Mrs. Rombi reported that the whole atmosphere of their home seemed calmer and more conducive to normal emotional reactions in Clara. The semester started out well with Clara carrying English II, science II, mathematics II and Latin I.

A report of Clara's work at the end of the first month follows:

English.—There is a little improvement but her attitude is one of trying to make a good impression rather than a desire to learn any subject matter. Her improvement seems entirely superficial.

Science II.—A noticeable breaking down in effort during the last week. She is not a poor student but uncertain in her effort. Any improvement she makes seems to be lacking in permanency.

Latin I.—Last year Clara had all the work which we are now covering. The second exposure is rather simple for her yet she only ranks in the middle of the class on power tests. In my class she exhibits a subtle repression which is hard for me to analyze.

Almost at the same time as the above reports came to the office, several men on the faculty reported that they were being annoyed each evening from seven to eight o'clock by anonymous telephone calls from a high-school girl. One of the men suspected that the girl was Clara and spoke to her the next morning. She denied it absolutely but explained in great detail that she knew who the girl was who was doing it; that the girl had great power of imitation; that she was unhappy at home and did not go out much and considered the whole episode a great lark. After the telephoning had gone on for about ten days, the instructor felt that Clara should either persuade the girl to confess and to stop her practice or that Clara should reveal the name of the girl who was guilty. Clara put the instructor off from day to day until the worker in the case in the presence of Clara and the instructor brought proof that she herself was guilty. When she had confessed, she lightly passed off the whole episode by saying, "Oh, all girls do that when they are unhappy and are, perhaps, boy crazy." There was no evidence of embarrassment or regret and there was no weighing or considering of the right or wrong involved in the situation.

Conference with the mother brought to light exactly what had been suspected, namely, that home conditions were worse again. Mr. Rombi was not well and most of his nervous irritability was directed toward Clara. It seemed clear that a correction of Clara's behavior could not be made as long as she stayed in the home. Mrs. Rombi was advised to send her to a school where the head mistress would understand the trouble and would be capable of giving corrective work. The advice was followed.

No happier individual could have been found than Clara when she learned that she was going away from home. For the first time in a year and a half she talked seriously and intelligently about her school work. Suddenly, she seemed to have been brought back to earth and was aware of her problems. She showed eagerness to settle down to an earnest piece of work. She thanked various members of the school again and again for their help and she was full of promises for the future. Was this just another form of compensation?

FOLLOW UP

Clara attended the boarding school until she graduated from high school. During this period she was sent to a girls' camp during the summer vacation so that she was in the home less than five weeks each year.

The following report was received from the boarding school after Clara had been in attendance there for a year and four months:

Subjects	Grades*
Modern history	B
English	B
French	C
History of art	C
Typewriting	C
Piano	B
Voice	B
Physical education	B

Social Qualities

Reactions in trying situations	B	
Leadership	B	
Courtesy	A	
Dignity of conduct	A	
Health habits	A	

Classroom Habits .... B

Cottage Habits

a. Room order	A
b. Taste in room	A
c. Consideration for cottage mates	A
d. Care and use of property	A
e. Performance of cottage regulations	B

* Definition of grades: A to B—, unqualified recommendation for college entrance examinations; C to C—, qualified recommendation; D to E, permission to take college entrance examinations will be denied.

Although Clara did not make an outstandingly excellent scholastic record, nevertheless, she did better than average in her courses. She was not a failure. Even more gratifying than school work was the marked social adjustment as evidenced by her attitude toward her cottage mates and in her reaction to regulations and by her conduct in a trying situation. As soon as she was relieved from the stress and strain of the disharmony in the home, she ceased to be a problem either socially or scholastically. She proved to herself that she could maintain her position with her equals and she began to enjoy the feeling of freedom from load and the comfortableness of security.

PROGNOSIS

The outlook is hopeful because social and scholastic adjustment has been made before Clara has outgrown the period of adolescence. It may be questioned whether she will be able to endure the friction of the home again when she returns. Two factors give promise and hope for future success. First, Clara herself is older and should be better equipped to cope with the trying situation; second, the report is that Mr. Rombi has begun to take a little parental pride in the accomplishment of his daughter, because Clara is physically very attractive, she has great poise, and she is socially very acceptable. The freedom of social conduct for which she longed is now being enjoyed. With it has come the feeling of adequacy and security. Wasteful daydreaming and overcompensation are no longer necessary.

CHAPTER VI

VOLITIONAL RETARDATION: THE CASE OF MARIAN MITCHEL

MARIAN MITCHEL, aged fourteen years and nine months, was a sophomore who had taken her freshman work in another high school. From the beginning of the school year her adjustment to the new situation appeared difficult, for it was evident that her class work was not being finished in a satisfactory manner and that social contacts were hard for her to make.

INVESTIGATION OF PRESENT SCHOOL LIFE

In a program consisting of English II, Spanish II, mathematics II and biology, English alone was being carried by her at a fairly acceptable level. Reports from Marian's instructors consistently emphasized certain definite facts. First, she gave evidence of more than average ability; second, she seemed to lack the drive and force to complete a task; third, she completed her work rather well if she had the personal attention of the teacher or was given an opportunity to lean on some other pupil; fourth, it was necessary to assign to her one small task at a time; fifth, upon finishing a task she sat idle until another bit of work was given; sixth, she was well-behaved, courteous in manner, and serious and well-intentioned; seventh, whenever any deficiency in work was brought to Marian's attention, she was quick to answer, "Yes, Mother is coming. She will explain."

Tests

Marian's I.Q. as determined by the Otis Higher Examination Test was 113. It is worthy of mention at this point that she did not answer as many questions in this test as she might have done, due to the fact that she was slow in getting started. Therefore she was given the test at a later date with no time limit. From the second test her I.Q. was computed to be 123.

An analysis of the test showed that there was weakness in the questions involving reasoning, in number sequences and the questions on general background. She made such mistakes in her answer as: "Tokyo is a city in China"; "Rodin is a famous painter."

Results of reading tests for both comprehension and speed placed Marian above average.

The Inglis vocabulary test showed no definite weakness but, on the contrary, a wide spread in various fields.

The Reavis-Breslich Diagnostic Tests in arithmetic showed average ability in arithmetic. Her score was 62. The median for her group was 60.14.

Present Physical Condition

A thorough examination by both the school and family physicians revealed definite physical handicaps:

Her vision was defective and glasses were recommended. There was a history and present evidence of chronic appendicitis. The tonsils were large, cryptic and buried and there was a tendency toward colds. The heart was a little rapid. Weight was fourteen pounds above the norm for her age and height.

Social Record in School

Her social life in school was exceedingly limited. Girls' Club activities, dances and athletic work were not entered into with sufficient ease and frequency to make them a source of pleasure. She had a small number of speaking acquaintances because she had a friendly attitude, but there were only two girls who could be called intimate friends. With these girls she appeared very childish in her levity and would burst into uncontrolled giggling and raucous laughter quite out of harmony with her general courteous bearing. She displayed little ability to enter into and carry on the ordinary "give and take" of adolescent conversation. In school social situations she was awkward, diffident, shy and retiring. A check on her personality traits placed emphasis on the following characteristics: negative in character, lethargic, apathetic, dilatory, self-conscious, intermittent, taciturn, unsociable but friendly.

Parents' Version of the Difficulty

Mrs. Mitchel stated that in former years Marian had always done work above the average and that she had no explanation for the lack of success in the present situation. She made the suggestion, however, that Marian probably would do better work if the instructors would only assign some tasks outside of class on which the mother could give special help. She could not help in Spanish but she felt competent to give her assistance in the other three subjects. The instructors had refused to give her the class material. In fact, they had insisted that Marian assume complete responsibility for her own work.

Marian's Story

Marian had thought that school was rather a pleasant place until this year. She had never worried about her work, she had always passed and if any difficulty had arisen, her mother had been able to adjust matters. She liked this school and the girls whom she knew but she was worried because she did not seem able to get her work finished as the others did. The instructors were kind and offered assistance when she asked for it but everything in class was different. She had no lessons to take home and to learn. The instructors expected her to do her own work independently and she just could not do it. When asked if she felt happy in school affairs she was a bit hesitant and then shyly replied, "I sometimes think that I should like to go to school parties but then, on the other hand, I am glad that I do not go because I never know what to say to people. I don't know how I should ever talk to a boy!"

During one of the numerous interviews with Marian and her mother, Mrs. Mitchel in apparent distress kept up a rapid fire of questions, "Marian, *why* don't you pass in your work? Don't you pay attention? You know that I cannot help you with Spanish. Won't your instructors help you? Is it their fault? Why don't you work? Why don't you try?" Quite unexpectedly and in contrast to her former placidity, Marian burst forth passionately, "But, Mother, you know I *can't*. I just *can't*. You know I can't." Those words were a pitiable cry of agony, the despairing wail of a youngster faced with a difficult situation out of which she saw no way. Mother had failed her and she knew not where to turn.

Interpretation

There are some very positive factors in the findings to date. Marian is above average in intelligence; she has good command of the tool subjects and she has an excellent vocabulary. There are, on the other hand, many influences which might account for Marian's weak attack on her work. The need for glasses, the distress caused by chronic appendicitis, infected tonsils with their toxic poisoning and overweight form a powerful combination of inhibiting physical causes. There is evidence of lack of volition expressed by the words, "I can't."

INVESTIGATION OF LIFE OUTSIDE OF SCHOOL

Marian is an only child. The regularity of her meals, the adequacy of diet, and sufficiency of sleep have always been matters of the greatest importance to the entire household. The fact is that routine and regularity are almost a fetish in this house. Even exercise is definitely and efficiently planned and consists of walks and games with a nurse or the mother. There is no time allotted for free play with companions.

As far as could be ascertained this only child had never been given any task to do in the home. The very clothes she was to wear were laid out ready to be put on every morning. She was actually dressed by the nurse until she was twelve years old. The nurse boasted that Marian had never bought a thing without supervision. She did not know what it was to do an errand or to be responsible for doing anything for anybody not even for herself. "She has been beautifully cared for and reared," is the comment of the mother.

Although there is a great deal of company in the house, the guests are usually adults so that contacts with young girls and boys are meager and limited to school situations.

The home shows every evidence of culture and breeding, and apparently there is a comfortable income. The library is extensive; magazines are of the better class, and pictures are well selected.

Mr. and Mrs. Mitchel are of German and Swedish stock. On both sides there is school training beyond the high school, the mother having had several years of college and the father having graduated from a small sectarian school. Mrs. Mitchel, a rather powerful woman, somewhat overdressed and rouged, appears to dominate the household, not rudely but, nevertheless, effectively. The father is a quiet, pleasant and courteous listener.

Interpretation

Although this home is far above average in background and physical comforts it is inadequate in helping the child to develop normally. The girl is so sheltered and so carefully cared for by an overzealous mother that there has always been a dearth of opportunity for Marian to develop initiative, no chance for her to do anything for herself, and no training in responsibility to others.

Pregnancy and birth were reported as normal. Shortly after birth the baby presented a feeding problem, and a nurse trained as a dietitian was brought into the household. Entire charge of the baby's meals—seeing that they were well-balanced and adequate—was taken over by this specialist. Marian's growth, teething and walking were normal. When she was twelve years old the nurse was still a member of the household and doing practically the same tasks which she had performed for her as a baby. Under this régime Marian had always been the center of attention. Every wish had been anticipated and gratified almost before it was expressed.

Emotional History

From earliest childhood the mother had been very particular about the child's associates. Only certain children from certain families were acceptable. Whenever a new playmate was brought into the home there was always a question as to whether the child was socially satisfactory. By evaluation of companions and by comments made by the mother Marian soon came to the realization that she was considered different and a little superior to most children from most families.

Shyness and diffidence were noticed early in life but Mrs. Mitchel had paid little attention to these characteristics, thinking that the child would outgrow the difficulties because of her inheritance and the many advantages she was to have.

As the child grew older, if there was not almost immediate gratification of a desire she did not go into a tantrum as some children do, but instead sulked and sat quietly doing nothing. The parents never could bear to see her unhappy so they made every attempt to foresee just what the child wished.

School attendance usually gives the necessary freedom for development to children from homes of this type. But it has not been so in this case. Marian is driven to and from school. At dismissal either the mother or the nurse are always to be seen hovering around the school building until Marian is ready to go home. This procedure has continued up to the present and Marian is a young lady in the second year of high school.

Mrs. Mitchel in her eagerness to gratify every wish had become the buffer for every situation. Every path was made smooth so that difficulties were never faced and realities were never met. Some one else was always at fault, never Marian. At the age of fourteen, if Marian were at school and it was necessary that a decision be made about even the most trivial matter, she did not know what to do or where to turn until she had telephoned home and asked what was the proper procedure.

School History

Until the second year in high school, Marian had attended the conventional public school. In her eight years of attendance at the same elementary school she had completed grade after grade without a failure. From an interview with a former teacher it became apparent that shyness and diffidence had characterized her social attitudes from the earliest grades. To the outsider there had never seemed to be a decided like or dislike for school on Marian's part. The whole situation had been accepted by her as another bit of routine which rounded out her well-ordered and efficiently managed life. Mrs. Mitchel had always been a frequent visitor in the school and, in her own words, she "had always been most co-operative with the teachers and had been able to control and adjust matters."

At a few months past thirteen years, Marian entered the public high school, and from the marks below it would seem as if she had carried her freshman course successfully.

Subjects	First Semester	Second Semester
English	87	92
Spanish	81	86
Algebra	75	80
Science	75	80

DIAGNOSIS

Primary Causation.—Marian is volitionally retarded, that is, she lacks the drive and motive power which are necessary to carry a task through to successful results. She is still clinging to the adaptive mechanisms which served her during the infantile stage of absolute dependency. In other words, this is a case of prolonged babyishness.

Contributory Causations.—(a) The change from a conventional type of school to a progressive school has emphasized initiative and independence. (b) Chronic appendicitis and infected tonsils which sap her vitality and cause a rapid heart tend also to lessen her drive and energy. The need for glasses complicates the class situation.

Support of Diagnosis

Through tests administered there is positive evidence that Marian has ability to do work of average quality at least, so that failure should not result in any subject. It is granted that the physical condition is poor and may well account for lethargy, apathy and slowness in attack, but it is not the root of indecision, self-consciousness and social inefficiency. The fault is more fundamental and is manifestly traceable to the fact that this home, from the infancy of the child, has given direct training in keeping her from outgrowing normally the infantile stage.

Every individual in growing from infancy to adulthood must go through a definite process of development in order that he may be freed from the state of absolute dependency and the normal egocentric tendency to complete indulgence and to existence without effort. As Doctor William White says: "He must break away from his infantile moorings, go forth into the world of reality and win there a place for himself."[1] There must be also a progressive tendency to project oneself upon objects of interest other than self, especially upon the persons of one's social environment.

The efficient domination of a supposedly intelligent mother has kept Marian in a sheltered home, shielded her from the hard knocks of life and provided her with no opportunity either to experience even the smallest amount of independence or to develop her own methods of attack on scholastic or social problems. Forced to focus her

[1] W. W. White, *Mechanisms of Character Formation* (The Macmillan Co., 1926), p. 147.

attention on herself she early and unconsciously, no doubt, set up barriers between herself and other human beings. Therefore, at fourteen years of age she was definitely retarded in the ability to mingle comfortably and happily with her companions.

Most children before they start to go to school have learned to dress themselves, to take their baths unassisted and to find their way about the neighborhood. Marian has been deprived of even this simple training. Furthermore, she has never experienced the keen desire for something for which she has had to work hard. Instead, wishes have been anticipated and gratified before they have been fully expressed. In short, she has been robbed of the very discipline that is an essential factor in making a strong, independent and responsible young person.

When Marian complained bitterly, "I can't," she expressed the actual fact. She could not! Put upon her own initiative she was similar to a baby attempting to walk. One could scarcely expect her to step out and walk alone on her first venture. Marian must learn first to stand alone, then, to walk a bit without the help and support of mother and teachers, and finally, to step out into new paths on her own initiative. Until the ingrained feeling of dependency has been eradicated and in its place a feeling of self-sufficiency established, there is little hope of Marian's succeeding in either school work or social contacts. Doctor Rank states: "The detachment of the growing individual from the control and authority of the parents is one of the most necessary but one of the most painful achievements of evolution. It is absolutely necessary for this detachment to take place, and it may be assumed that all normal grown individuals have accomplished it to a certain extent."[2]

Without a doubt, the exciting agent to this immediate difficulty was the change from a conventional type of school to a progressive institution which stressed individual work, independence and initiative. This change brought a complete breakdown because the qualities emphasized in the new situation were the very ones which she had not developed and in which she was abnormally retarded. Furthermore, there is a definite physical condition powerful enough because of systemic poisoning to enervate the individual and to aggravate the natural disposition not to exert oneself.

TREATMENT

Before remedial work was started on the fundamental difficulty it was thought advisable to remove as far as possible all physical causes of lack of energy. Glasses were fitted immediately. During a short holiday the tonsils were removed without any disturbing effects. After the removal of the tonsils the physician stated that the condition of the appendix was not serious enough to warrant an operation at this time.

Remedial work in this case means reëducation of both the parents and the girl. In Marian, habits of a lifetime must be broken down. Mrs. Mitchel must be made to realize that her daughter's difficulties are due to the prolonged spoiling process of the home. It is no small task to convince parents that a child is spoiled and that

[2] O. Rank, *The Myth of the Birth of a Hero*, Nervous and Mental Disease Monograph Series, No. 18.

in volitional development she is still an infant. Most people recognize physical and mental retardation, but few are convinced that volitional retardation even exists. In their opinions the will-to-do is inherent in every *good* child and develops effectively without any training. Only naughty children do not know how to settle down and perform required tasks. Even if parents grant that they have spoiled a child, few have the grit to turn right about face and attempt to remedy the matter.

With much persuasion, Mrs. Mitchel consented to co-operate in every detail with the suggestions of the school. Careful explanation was given that only through concrete tasks set and constantly checked up could Marian gain self-confidence. She must learn to do by doing and by exerting herself independently.

Periods of discouragement and lapses in effort were many and yet they were to be expected. Although progress was very slow it was noticeable almost immediately.

The first request made was that Marian should select the dress she was to wear, dress herself and walk to and from school. The mother was so foolish about the latter request that for almost a week she hovered in the distance, driving far enough behind Marian not to be seen but near enough to watch her. Walking to and from school had a most wholesome effect, for Marian fell in with different groups of girls and boys, and it soon became evident that she was forming friendships normally and naturally. The work with Marian was much easier than with the mother. Mrs. Mitchel thought that we were cruel and heartless when we insisted that Marian go down town alone and select a new outfit unassisted. At another time there was active resentment shown because Marian was breaking the ties and really growing up. Mrs. Mitchel complained that "the school was robbing her of her child." The shock and disappointment that Marian was picking up the habits and vernacular of the ordinary child were at times convincing to the mother that our plan was not the best one.

Instructors in classroom and in extracurricular activities helped whole-heartedly and untiringly in assisting Marian to find herself and to succeed. Encouragement, patience but firmness on the part of her teachers made her realize that she could achieve results comparable to her classmates. Class-work improved, and with extra assistance in opportunity classes she completed the work of the sophomore year with full credit. Through clubs and gymnasium work she was brought into the play life of the normal girl. A position on a third class hockey team was heralded as a big step in advance. It was, in fact, a greater achievement for Marian than a place on an all-star team for the average girl in the school.

When Marian of her own volition came in to discuss her program for the junior year, she proved that the training was bringing results. She had ideas of her own and was making plans for going to college. In most girls in high school this would be nothing out of the ordinary but it spelled confidence in Marian's case. She was learning to walk alone. Slowly but surely independence, initiative and self-confidence were established.

FOLLOW UP

Marian graduated from high school and spent two years in college away from home. Socially she was retiring and reserved but she was not considered "queer" and different. One could not expect a brilliant scholastic record, but she did work of average grade and experienced no failures.

CHAPTER VII

DEPRESSION: THE CASE OF GERTRUDE TURNER

GERTRUDE TURNER, aged thirteen years, entered high school from a public elementary school. The case came to the attention of the worker because of the marked contrast between Gertrude's record in the eighth grade and the quality of her work in high school. At first she seemed to be adjusting herself to the new conditions without difficulty, but within two months she was in distress in all subjects.

INVESTIGATION OF PRESENT SCHOOL LIFE

Instructors' reports follow:

Mathematics.—Gertrude is failing in mathematics in spite of the great amount of additional help which has been given to her. Her difficulty does not seem to be due to inability as much as to the fact that she does not assume responsibility for getting the work done. At times she has demonstrated keen mathematical insight.

French.—Gertrude is having decided difficulty with her French. I am wondering if the difficulty is not more with Gertrude than with the French. She seems to lack the will-to-do. Her attention is not concentrated on the problem of the classroom. It will require all the initiative and application she can summon for her to succeed.

Science.—Gertrude is just barely meeting our requirements

in this course. She has failed to make a real effort and consequently she is usually behind the class. She has ability, I can see, but she does not seem to be able to muster her forces.

English.—Gertrude has required a great deal of reteaching. She has difficulty chiefly because she does not put her mind on what she is doing. Her mistakes are usually due to carelessness rather than to ignorance. She does not seem to force herself to study for any length of time. She seems interested in the course but she has not utilized that interest for effective work.

Art.—Gertrude is slow in getting at her work and she has great difficulty in giving her undivided attention to what she is doing. Her mind seems befogged at times. Her work is very mediocre in quality.

Tests

The Otis Higher Examination was given. According to that test Gertrude's I.Q. was 123.

DETAILED RESULTS OF REAVIS-BRESLICH DIAGNOSTIC TESTS IN THE FUNDAMENTAL OPERATIONS OF ARITHMETIC AND IN PROBLEM SOLVING

Test	Number Correct	Time Given, Minutes	Median, VIII A
Tests I—VIII			
Addition	6	3	
Subtraction	6	1.5	
Multiplication	6	3	
Division	3	4	
Addition and Subtraction of Fractions	7	2	
Multiplication and Division of Fractions	8	2	
Placing Decimal Point in Multiplication	9	1	
Placing Decimal Point in Division ...	5	1.5	
Score: I—VIII	50		38.53
Test IX: Problems without Numbers...	9	6	4.42
Test X: Problems with Numbers	9	4	8.16

RESULTS OF READING TESTS

Test	Gertrude's Score	Median, IX
Monroe Silent Reading Test		
Rate	130	122
Comprehension	64	46.4
Thorndike-McCall Reading Scale ...	80	67.5
Inglis Vocabulary	93	63.1

Physical Condition

Gertrude's physical record card showed little of significance. She had a slight heart murmur which kept her from too strenuous exercise but apparently affected her general health very little. Her weight was normal. Sleep was reported as interrupted and restless. The physical record card indicated that it usually took her a long time to go to sleep and, according to her statement, she dreamed a great deal.

Social Record in School

Gertrude was a very attractive, unsophisticated, charming girl. She was a favorite in her own group and was well liked by her classmates. As evidence of her popularity she had been elected vice-president of her class and had been appointed chairman of the social committee in the Art Club. One day in casual conversation one of her good friends made the remark, "Gertrude isn't one bit like her old self. She isn't as gay and happy as she used to be. I don't know what's the matter with her and I never can get her to talk about the trouble. I guess she is worried about the poor work that she has been doing recently in her classes for she has always been an honor student."

Version of Mother and Daughter

A poor school record was such an unheard-of situation in the Turner household that both Mrs. Turner and Gertrude were humble and apologetic. Gertrude was filled with shame and embarrassment. She said time and time again that she had the greatest desire to do well but just couldn't tell why she wasn't getting the work. She just couldn't account for herself. None of the work seemed hard, nevertheless, she didn't seem to do as well as the others. She felt that she was really trying. Her failures caused bitter weeping and much unhappiness.

Interpretation of Findings

In no part of the report is there any indication that Gertrude's failures are due to lack of mental ability or to inadequate preparation. The test scores are unusually high. The arithmetic score is equal to the median for the junior year in high school. Reading and vocabulary tests reveal no weaknesses, in fact, they not only prove the ability of the girl but they also show that she has had good preparation and previous training. The complaints of the instructors that "lack of attention, inability to force herself to work and ineffective habits of study" as characteristics of her classroom attitude might easily lead one to conclude that this is a volitional case, that Gertrude has capacity to do her work but that she is not sufficiently interested in attacking hard tasks to earn success. Yet, when one considers her feeling of shame, her distress because of failure and her apparent emotional upset one outrules any volitional cause and seeks further for the root of the serious inattention.

An indication of the reason for difficulty can be found in the physical record and the social life in school. Gertrude does not sleep well. She lies awake for a long time each night. Rest does not come easily. This factor may be producing an enervating weariness and fatigue which make concentration on work impossible. This sleeplessness must be accounted for as it is not natural for a healthy young person to suffer with insomnia. There is in addition a definite social change. Her best friend has observed it even though Gertrude has never discussed matters with her. Spontaneous gayety has gone, and her good friend believes that low grades are the cause of the depression. One is convinced at this point that there is something working underneath which has not yet come to light but which is causing loss of sleep, change in social attitude and poor school work.

INVESTIGATION OF LIFE OUTSIDE OF SCHOOL

Gertrude was an only child of parents who had passed middle life. In the home there had been little contact with girls and boys of Gertrude's age, in fact, most of her recreation had been taken in the company of her relatives and their friends. In discussing the home situation with Mrs. Turner special inquiry was made about Gertrude's statement that she could not sleep. The mere question seemed to stir Mrs. Turner emotionally and she appeared hesitant to reply. At last she revealed this story. Gertrude had had very bad nights for some time. A cousin, Mrs. Palmer, and her husband, a newly-married couple, had lived in the apartment below the Turners' and had been a part of the Turner home life. Gertrude had been with Mrs. Palmer almost as much as she had been in her own home. Suddenly and unexpectedly Mr. Palmer had died. In her sorrow the wife had turned to Gertrude and had wanted to have the girl with her constantly so that night after night Gertrude had served as an outlet for the cousin's grief. Unfortunately Gertrude's bedroom was directly above Mrs. Palmer's, and even though she slept in her own home she was often kept awake by the sobbing and crying of her cousin. Mrs. Turner confessed that she had noticed that Gertrude appeared tired in the morning and that lately she seemed to talk of little else than her cousin's loss. Mr. Palmer's death was the first in Gertrude's immediate family and it had made a deep impression upon her. Mrs. Turner had begun to realize that the whole home situation was an unwholesome one for her daughter but she had felt powerless to correct it.

A conference with Gertrude brought out more clearly the serious affects the tragedy had had upon her. She had been very fond of Mr. Palmer and she had felt his death very keenly. Furthermore, it worried her that Mrs. Palmer was left alone in the world and there seemed to be so little one could do. Not only was she grief-stricken but she was burdened with the responsibility of giving sufficient comfort to her cousin. Everything now seemed so gloomy, sad and depressing.

EARLY DEVELOPMENTAL HISTORY

There was nothing of significance in this period except her school record. Gertrude had been an honor student throughout the grade school. Her eighth-grade report contained superior grades in all subjects. Special notation was made on her excellence in mathematics. Her recommendation to high school was the best in her group.

DIAGNOSIS

Primary Causation.—The primary cause of Gertrude's condition is an emotional perversion, in the form of depression, which exerts such a strong inhibitory action that the pupil's whole attention is so completely absorbed that the mind has not been free to cope with the classroom problems.

Secondary Causation.—This is clearly weariness and fatigue, caused by worry and loss of sleep lowering the resistance to distractions in the classroom.

Support of Diagnosis

"Mental hygienists are stressing one great point that in most cases of nervousness, and in many cases of behavior or conduct disorders, the trail leads inevitably and directly back to the home."[1] A glimpse into the family life reveals and accounts for all sorts of emotional perversions in adolescent girls. All these perversions appear in school as conduct. Whenever a case-worker has a conduct case to handle he can usually decide that there is one or more of these emotional perversions working now or in the past history. One must also keep in mind that it is difficult for any one to do any work of any kind during an emotional upset because everything at that time is out of perspective. Interest is one of the biggest, most powerful emotional drives we have. When one is

[1] George K. Pratt, M.D., *A Mental Health Primer* (National Committee for Mental Hygiene, 370 Seventh Ave., New York City).

worried, bothered or troubled there can be no interest in work because the whole emotional mechanism is occupied with something else.

The case in hand illustrates this very principle. The death of Mr. Palmer had made a very deep impression upon Gertrude. Not only was it the first time she had experienced the loss of a dear one but she had been called upon to assume the burden of reconciling and comforting Mrs. Palmer. The death was in itself, no doubt, sufficient shock to produce a slackening in mental activity but the responsibility which she felt toward Mrs. Palmer was overwhelming. She did not seem equal to the task and she thought about it all the time. The morbid emotional condition gripped her completely and kept her in a preoccupied state. Her interest and drive were spent in trying to solve something to which she could find no solution.

Naturally a keen, intelligent student the lowering of the school record had worried her more and more. But she seemed powerless to struggle against the waves of depression and to meet the demands made upon her. Instead of getting normal relief from the depression by a good night's rest, she was plunged further into despair by long protracted conversations with her cousin. In such a manner a vicious circle was established, and she was never left wholly free emotionally nor fresh mentally to attack her school problems. Truly everything was out of perspective.

TREATMENT AND PROGNOSIS

The diagnosis of Gertrude's difficulty was explained carefully to Mrs. Turner and it was made very clear to her that Gertrude's morbid, emotional condition would not be changed to a normal attitude unless Gertrude was removed from the gloomy atmosphere in the home. Very definite instructions were given: (1) Under no circumstances was Gertrude to be left alone with Mrs. Palmer. (2) There should be a change in rooms so that Mrs. Palmer's demonstrations of grief could not be heard. (3) By physician's prescription a mild sedative should be administered so that a sound, refreshing sleep could be assured. (4) Mrs. Palmer should be made aware of Gertrude's condition. (5) Young companions should be brought into the home and the social life should be made gay and happy. (6) If possible, the summer should be spent out in the open away from her immediate family.

The mother was most coöperative and every effort was made to carry out the remedial suggestions.

It is very rare that a case clears up as quickly as this one did. There were immediate and almost miraculous results. As soon as Gertrude talked the matter out, it was as if a heavy burden had dropped from her shoulders. Relief came quickly. To alleviate the whole situation Mrs. Palmer was called to a distant city on business so that the most distressing element in the home was removed.

At school one subject was dropped so that all effort could be directed toward ending the year successfully.

After a summer in the country Gertrude returned in excellent health and fine spirits. During her sophomore year she carried with honor English II, French II, mathe-matics III and history. From no instructor was there anything but the highest commendation for Gertrude's attention and attainment.

Four years of high school and four years of college were completed without further difficulty.

CHAPTER VIII

INSECURITY: THE CASE OF LILLIAN PAGE

LILLIAN entered the first year of high school from an excellent boarding school for young girls. She was thirteen years old. Her classes for the freshman year were English, mathematics, Latin and science.

One day Lillian appeared in the office, sullen, rebellious and on the verge of tears. An instructor had sent her from class because for two days she had refused to answer any questions he asked.

INVESTIGATION OF PRESENT SCHOOL LIFE

All instructors without exception reported that Lillian was uncommunicative, appeared burdened, unhappy and discontented. They did not seem able to tell whether she did not have ability or whether she just would not work. She took no part in any class group work, she refused to follow directions and she appeared to resent any advances on the part of the instructors to get acquainted and to help. She was failing in mathematics, Latin and science, for she had done no part of the work completely.

Tests

In the Pintner Non-Language Mental Test Lillian's score gave her a mental index of 66. According ·to the norms this score placed her in the bright group or upper 25 per cent.

According to her score in the Otis Higher Examination (*A* Test) her I.Q. was 109.

In the reading and arithmetic tests she scored as follows:

· Test	Lillian's Score	Median, IX
Monroe Silent Reading Test (Comprehension): Test III (Form I)	27	25.4 ·
Burgess Silent Reading Scale ·........	63	58
Thorndike-McCall Reading Scale	64	66.1
Inglis Vocabulary	51	45.6
Reavis-Breslich Diagnostic Tests in Fundamental Operations of Arithmetic and in Problem Solving......	50	52.2

In the last test, there is evidence of weakness in Part IX, Problems without Numbers. In taking this section of the test she read the directions but seemed to pay little heed to them. She remarked that she could not do the problems because there were no numbers. Explanation was made that she merely had to tell what processes she would use. She remained silent, read through the problems but made no move to do any of them. In all other operations she showed normal accomplishment.

Downey Individual Will-Temperament Test

This chart shows Lillian to be an inhibited, unaggressive individual with little confidence and decision. Indi-

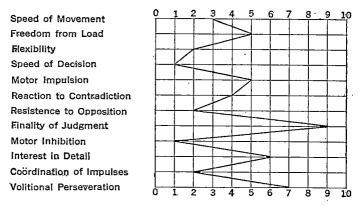

Speed of Movement
Freedom from Load
Flexibility
Speed of Decision
Motor Impulsion
Reaction to Contradiction
Resistence to Opposition
Finality of Judgment
Motor Inhibition
Interest in Detail
Coördination of Impulses
Volitional Perseveration

RECORD CARD OF DOWNEY INDIVIDUAL WILL-TEMPERAMENT TEST
Devised by June E. Downey, Ph.D. (World Book Co., Publishers, Yonkers-on-Hudson, New York).

cations are that she feels inferior. She repeatedly declared her inability to do certain parts of the test, some of which she did, however, very creditably. She needed constant urging to put forth her best effort.

Present Physical Condition

A very thorough physical examination was given by the family physician and checked by the school physician. It was shown that Lillian's sight was normal, her hearing and nutrition excellent, her pulse when sitting was 68, and following exercise, 92. Her general condition was described as follows: "She is an unusually strong and well-developed young adolescent. She shows no physical weakness nor any diseased condition."

Social Record in School

Contacts with her schoolmates were few since Lillian participated rarely in extracurricular activities. A chauffeur left her at the door of the school each morning and called for her at dismissal so that all natural and simple contacts gained in walking to and from school in the

COMPOSITE PERSONALITY ESTIMATE OF FIVE TEACHERS

	High		Medium		Low		
Refined			x				Coarse
Democratic						x	Snobbish
Cheery						x	Peevish
Patient						x	Irritable
Courteous						x	Discourteous
Friendly						x	Reserved
Cordial						x	Indifferent
Sociable						x	Unsociable
Imaginative						x	Prosaic
Altruistic						x	Selfish
Coöperative						x	Combative
Open-to-suggestion				x			Opinionated
Optimistic						x	Pessimistic
Contented						x	Dissatisfied
Keenly alive						x	Apathetic
Loquacious						x	Taciturn
Self-poised			x				Flighty
Calm		x					Excitable
Trustful					x		Jealous
Well-spoken					x		Gossipy
Common-sense							Lacking in judgment
Frank					x		Underhanded
Honest			x				Dishonest
Reliable						x	Unreliable
Reasonable						x	Unreasonable
Prompt						x	Dilatory
Industrious						x	Idle
Attentive						x	Inattentive
Steady						x	Intermittent

group were lost. In the gymnasium she seemed a bit more confident and sure of herself and entered into all sports and exercise with some display of interest. To

FATHER'S ESTIMATE OF LILLIAN'S PERSONALITY

	High		Medium		Low	
Refined		x				Coarse
Democratic			x			Snobbish
Cheery		x				Peevish
Patient		x				Irritable
Courteous		x				Discourteous
Friendly				x		Reserved
Cordial			x			Indifferent
Sociable			x			Unsociable
Imaginative	x					Prosaic
Altruistic		x				Selfish
Coöperative		x				Combative
Open-to-suggestion			x			Opinionated
Optimistic			x			Pessimistic
Contented			x			Dissatisfied
Keenly alive			x			Apathetic
Loquacious				x		Taciturn
Self-poised		x				Flighty
Calm					x	Excitable
Trustful						Jealous
Well-spoken		x	x			Gossipy
Common-sense		x				Lacking in judgment
Frank			x			Underhanded
Honest		x				Dishonest
Reliable		x				Unreliable
Reasonable			x			Unreasonable
Prompt		x				Dilatory
Industrious		x				Idle
Attentive		x				Inattentive
Steady		x				Intermittent

the girls in the gymnasium class Lillian was merely "retiring and quiet" in contrast to the impression she created in other classes of being "queer and dumb."

Parent's Version of the Difficulty

Frequent conferences with Mr. Page gave very little assistance in the case. He was at a loss to explain failure in class work and the antagonistic attitude which was displayed in school. Although she had never been an outstanding student, failure was unknown to her. At home she was doing exceedingly well in her music. Two to three hours of practice a day were not unusual and there was no need for urging on his part. His estimate of her personality was based on her steady interest and determined attack on her music. As he expressed it, "Lillian is herself when she is at the piano. She is creative, imaginative and at complete ease."

Lillian's Version of the Difficulty

To get an explanation of any difficulties from Lillian was next to impossible. No one connected with the school seemed able to make any sort of friendly approach. Lillian resented the conferences, in fact, she appeared to resent every person and everything connected with the classroom. A shrug of her shoulders, a nod of the head or mere monosyllabic replies were the responses given to any question or query. Lillian simply would not talk. She sat silently and looked as it were not from her eyes but from behind her eyes as if she were weighing deliberately what defense she should make. The sad, unhappy look, however, belied her appearance of combative defiance. The most tactful and diplomatic approach never seemed to break down the reserve until one day when a preponderous amount of evidence of lack of coöperation and failure was presented, Lillian, without any warning, burst forth vehemently, "What's the matter? What have they against *me?* I'm always getting penalty cards. I work just as hard, if not harder than my sister, and I do just as well as she does but she hasn't received one criticism this whole year. I don't belong here and I don't want to stay. I don't know where I belong."

Interpretation

Information on the tests would indicate that this is a learning case which has grown out of a conduct case. Lillian is not what is ordinarily termed a discipline case in school, but there is every indication of serious difficulties especially in attitude. The Downey-Will Temperament Test defines her as one who is exceedingly inhibited and unaggressive. Her extreme taciturnity, unapproachableness and combativeness all point to some deep-seated emotion. The one outburst in the office and the remark about her sister's success as contrasted with her own might be interpreted on the one hand as a feeling of jealousy, or on the other as a feeling of inequality or insecurity. There is a marked difference in the composite estimate of her instructors and that made by her father. To the latter Lillian is cheery, patient, imaginative, coöperative, optimistic, contented, prompt, industrious, attentive and steady, *exceedingly excitable;* to her instructors she is peevish, irritable, prosaic, combative, pessimistic, dissatisfied, dilatory, idle, inattentive, intermittent and *calm*—quite a different picture in two situations.

INVESTIGATION OF LIFE OUTSIDE OF SCHOOL

As has been stated before Lillian was a fine physical specimen who showed the effects of care in bringing up. The Page family was one of great wealth and social prominence. The father was a banker of no ordinary reputation and had come from a family of wealth and culture for many previous generations. In addition, Mr. Page was a kindly, understanding human sort of gentleman. Mrs. Page, who died when Lillian was about four years old, had also been well bred and well educated.

The home was large, beautifully furnished and adequately equipped with servants. Moreover, it was a real home with an atmosphere of refinement, comfortableness and general cordiality. Everything about it represented stability, serenity and social security.

All members of the family—father, Sarah, the older sister, Lillian and the maternal grandmother—were affable, congenial and companionable. The grandmother had lived with the family for about two years. Sarah Page was a vivacious, sociable and popular girl who was wholly acceptable to any social group and entered into every situation whole-heartedly.

Lillian's diversions were of a simple nature befitting her age and training. She enjoyed a few parties but received her greatest pleasure from concerts and operas, for music was her real interest in life.

Failures at school were not discussed in family conference. Mr. Page never permitted reference to be made to school work of this type. So Lillian was not subjected to odious comparisons and discouraging experiences. There was to all appearances no discordant note in this wholesome situation and one would have expected Lillian to be a happy, successful and interested pupil instead of the discontented, failing and sullen little person the school knew.

EARLY HISTORY AND DEVELOPMENT

Physical History

Mr. Page was non-committal and reticent whenever Lillian's early history was mentioned. Little information could be gained because when questions were asked, indefinite replies were given, such as, "Everything is all right," or "Lillian has always been a very fine specimen physically." When the school situation, however, continued to grow worse Mr. Page confided to the worker that Lillian was adopted when she was three years old. At the time of the adoption she had been examined by physicians and psychiatrists and had been pronounced physically strong and mentally very bright. On investigation into the background of the father and mother the records showed that both parents had come from clean, wholesome stock and were themselves hard-working, industrious and self-respecting people. Such detailed information as pregnancy, age of walking and talking could not be obtained.

Emotional History

Even after the adoption of Lillian had been divulged, Mr. Page gave little information concerning Lillian's early years with the family. Only the most patient and sympathetic probing brought forth the harrowing tale of Lillian's difficult adjustment to life from the age of three.

One day on the way to a train, Mrs. Page was being

driven through one of the poorest, most poverty-stricken sections of a large city. The street was blocked by excited women and yelling children. The center of attention seemed to be focused on the scuffling of a burly policeman and a three-year-old mite. The policeman was attempting to carry a kicking, clawing, scratching bit of humanity to a nearby patrol wagon. Shrieks, screams and piercing yells rent the air. The baby was a resisting little animal and the policeman was making little headway. Natural sympathy and mother love were aroused in Mrs. Page and she endeavored to find out the cause of the commotion. This was a difficult task because most of the women spoke a foreign language and they were far too excited to use the little English they chanced to know. Through persuasion Mrs. Page got the story from the policeman and she gained permission to take the child in her car to the police station. So goes the story. An epidemic had swept this section of the city. Scarcely a home had been untouched. During the epidemic both parents of Lillian had died. Incredible as it may seem, this little three-year-old child and her sister, two years older, had supported themselves for three days after the funeral from the refuse picked up on the street and from garbage cans. Cold and weak from lack of food, they were discovered by neighbors. At once the authorities were notified, and the scene just described was the result of the attempt to protect them. Lillian had resisted and fought, but the older sister had been docile and yielding. She had gone willingly with the policeman.

Through the proper channels Lillian was legally adopted by the Page family and she was provided with every necessity and luxury. A beautiful, attractive nursery was hers. A charming, understanding nursery governess was secured. But Lillian did not respond. She hated and feared all of them. She looked at people from behind her eyes as if she did not trust them and must be constantly on her guard. She never talked, was combative and acted much like a young animal which has been kicked about and is afraid. In the charming nursery she spent most of her waking hours under the bed. It was not an unusual thing for her meals to be served at the edge of the bed for days at a time.

The Pages had one daughter of their own but during the first three years of Lillian's life in the adopted family, there had been little normal contact between the two girls, although every effort was made by Sarah Page to show her love and affection for Lillian. Sarah had been delighted to have a little sister and when the dark, curly-headed baby had been brought into the home she had accepted her willingly and unconditionally.

During the first year of the adoption Mrs. Page had died and the full responsibility of bringing up Lillian had fallen upon Mr. Page. According to the father's story it had taken three years before the child had behaved like a normal human being. Gradually through patience, sympathetic understanding and no coercion she had responded to the father and the governess. Trust and confidence were restored and gradually Lillian became happy, animated and at times even joyous. She idolized Mr. Page and would do anything to please him. It was he who had discovered her talent in music and had provided her with every opportunity to express herself through this outlet. At the early age of seven she had spent voluntarily many hours in practicing. Music was always a source of joy to her. Mr. Page in turn was devoted to Lillian. He had much the same attitude toward her development as a gardener who has patiently cultivated and cared for a beautiful, delicate flower and has seen it come to full bloom.

After the information of Lillian's early life had been given to the school the father was told of Lillian's rebellious attitude toward the penalty cards and her statement, "I work just as hard if not harder than my sister and I do just as well as she does but she hasn't received one criticism this whole year. I don't belong here and I don't want to stay. I don't know where I belong."

Could he account for the complaints? He was astonished and said that he had had every reason to believe that Lillian had become well adjusted during the last four or five years. He could not fathom what had caused the setback at this time. For a week he studied the home situation intelligently and made the following significant report: For days Lillian had played an old melody over and over again. One evening she turned from the piano and unexpectedly remarked, "Whenever I play this piece I always think of you." Jokingly, Mr. Page replied, "Then, you have been thinking of me a great deal lately." "Yes," she said. "Father, I do belong to you, don't I?" He reassured her that she belonged particularly to him because he had wanted her badly enough to adopt her. Mr. Page also saw that although the maternal grandmother liked Lillian very much and never discriminated against her, she practically idolized Sarah and had said many, many times when the family was present, "Sarah, you grow to look more like your mother every day. You look just as she did when your father started to court

her. He surely must see the striking resemblance, too."
Innocent, unthinking remarks these were but they struck
a discordant note in Lillian's sensitive soul.

School History

All school work until the fourth grade had been carried
on in the home under the direction of a governess and
Mr. Page. At the age of nine, Lillian entered the fourth
grade in a small private school for little children. She
spent three years in this school. Lillian was ready for
the seventh grade when a business trip abroad made it
necessary for Mr. Page to be away from home for two
or three months during the school year. Lillian's adjustment seemed to be made and Mr. Page was anxious to put
her on her own for awhile so that she might have the
opportunity of gaining more independence. He was quite
aware of her utter devotion and dependence upon him.
Lillian spent the next two years in a small school for
girls in the East. Reports from the school were very
good. Although Lillian was not a leader in the classroom
she learned with ease. There was a decided reticence
in her behavior but this characteristic gave her an appearance of charm and poise and had in no way hindered
her progress. For two summers Lillian had been a member of a private camp for girls. She had enjoyed her
life to the full and had won high honors in swimming
and diving.

DIAGNOSIS

Primary Causation.—An emotional disturbance in the
form of an overwhelming feeling of insecurity had been
caused by a fight for existence in babyhood.

Secondary Causation.—The girl was utterly dependent upon her foster father.

Tertiary Causation.—The fear of losing her father had an inhibitory effect on her school work.

Contributory Causations.—Three contributory causes were (*a*) membership in the same school with Sarah; (*b*) strong resemblance of Sarah to her deceased mother; and (*c*) presence of the maternal grandmother in the home.

Support of Diagnosis

Born in the slums of a big city, Lillian had known only poverty and want as the background of her early years. From all accounts, the life of her parents had been a hard struggle for the necessities of a bare existence. The sudden loss of both parents must have been a terrific shock to these babies. Thrown absolutely upon their own resources they had fought for existence. Lillian, although the younger of the two, had displayed the greater initiative and energy for it was she who had done most of the foraging. For three whole days she had put up a struggle against the cold, hard facts of life. It was her fight, one can see, for *she* had strenuously resisted the policeman, while her sister had gone peacefully and docilely to the station. Everything for a few days had been insecure enough in the familiar surroundings of the old home but when suddenly a forbidding wagon had appeared to carry her away, she had clung desperately to the one familiar spot she had known. Hence, the terrific fight—the clawing and biting, the resistance to the force which was sweeping away everything which was known to her, everything which she felt was certain and sure.

One cannot overestimate the deep and lasting impression such a struggle had made upon the emotional life of the baby.

So great had been the shock and strain that even after she had been taken into a family of wealth which provided love and protection in abundance she could not be certain, she could not be free nor could she enjoy the material things provided. The fight had made her wary. The struggle had torn the very fibers of her being and the healing process was a long and slow one. In fear she had hidden under the bed, she had refused to come out into the open, she had been like a wounded animal which seeks to be alone in its suffering. Cramped, inhibited and fearful she had fought off affection. What had finally broken the chains of her horrible fear? It had been the gentle, understanding patience of Mr. Page. It had taken three years for him to win her trust, her confidence and her faith. Is it surprising that Lillian's whole life centered around him, that she grew utterly dependent upon him and that he represented all that was certain and constant? He had never failed her. Through his kindliness and his beautiful character all life had been opened to her.

Happiness, fearlessness and adjustment had lasted for five years and she had progressed successfully with the business of life which at her age is school.

At thirteen in school unhappy, sullen and unsuccessful —what had caused the change? What was at the basis of this reversion to the old-time fear? Only insecurity and uncertainty could bring about a second emotional upheaval. That uncertainty would probably be connected with her father and the loss of his affection and devotion. When Lillian said, "I don't belong in this school and I don't want to stay. I don't know where I belong," she gave definite evidence that the seeds of doubt had been sown once more. That old, gnawing, devastating fear of insecurity had her in its grip. What was it that made her feel that she did not know where she belonged?

In the home every day she saw Sarah, Mr. Page's *own* daughter, growing more and more like her mother. A feeling of jealousy was established, not jealousy of Sarah herself or her accomplishment in school but jealousy of Sarah's real claim to *her* foster father. Jealousy is always an admission to oneself of inferiority and inadequacy in the situation. More and more Sarah grew to look and act like her mother, the woman her father had loved enough to marry. To aggravate still more the open wound the maternal grandmother had come to live with them. She had not been a member of the group during Lillian's adjustment period. To Lillian the grandmother was an outsider but to Mr. Page and Sarah she was connected by a family bond—such a bond as Lillian did not have in common with them. The grandmother idolized Sarah for in her she saw again her own beautiful, young daughter. The likeness was remarkable, so remarkable that she thoughtlessly harped on it and reiterated the fact that Sarah looked as the mother did when Mr. Page began to court her. These remarks were salt on the open wound.

Lillian's one outlet was the piano. Over and over again she played the melody which made her think of her father. When she turned from the piano and said, "I do belong to you, don't I?" we probably have the outward expression of the severe inner struggle. Was the very foundation of things going from beneath her again? Would the father's entire affection be directed again to Sarah, the child of the woman he adored? Under this emotional strain how could school be anything more than a mere incident in the day's routine? All Lillian's energy was being consumed in a struggle for self-preservation and security. Interest in subject matter, attention, desire to learn were utterly wiped out by the turmoil which involved her whole emotional being. Where did she belong?

TREATMENT

How could a feeling of security and confidence be reestablished in Lillian? "Reëstablished" is used advisedly because it is certain that Lillian had felt that she belonged during the greater part of her elementary school years. Should Lillian be sent to a smaller school of which her sister was not a member? Should Lillian be sent to boarding school away from the home situation? Should remedial work be started in the home and the present school situation? These were big problems. Upon the answers to these questions rested the happiness and progress of a thirteen-year-old girl.

After thought and deliberation it was deemed wisest in this particular case to cope with the situation just as it was. Often a change of environment will relieve the emotional tension sufficiently to open the way to adjustment. In Lillian's case, however, unless there were internal changes, leaving her home would probably greatly exaggerate her emotion. She might feel that she had been cast from the fold.

Lillian herself must be given insight into her own difficulty. She had been adopted and Sarah was Mr. Page's own child. Nothing could ever change these facts. In every one's life there are certain facts which no one can change but which must be faced calmly and sensibly. The growing up process means that one has learned to take facts as they are and make adjustments to meet them. Unless Lillian herself could accept her adoption in a satisfactory way, all during her life circumstances would come up which would create the same complex with its resulting emotional disturbance.

All members of the household must sense the seriousness of the situation. Every effort must be made to give Lillian the assurance that she really belonged to the family, especially to the father, that she had been taken into the family group without a single reservation and that they all adored and loved her for herself and what she was.

There was need of consummate tact and thoughtfulness for Lillian was perfectly intelligent and was sensitive to all situations so that any crude false efforts would have proved disastrous.

Sarah had understanding quite beyond her years, and she did everything to show her real affection to Lillian. Extra attentions, talking over the school subjects, inclusion in a few simple social affairs, all helped to bring reassurance to Lillian.

The grandmother showed the least appreciation of the difficulty, but she did coöperate to the extent of refraining from constantly mentioning Mrs. Page and Sarah's resemblance to her. A convenient invitation for an extended trip with Mr. Page's sister brought the family back to the original "Happy Three," as Mr. Page called the trio.

By the same patient methods which Mr. Page had used in the early days of her adoption Lillian began again to feel the satisfying assurance of the deep affection which her father had for her. She realized the care and devotion he had given to her to draw her from the wretched fear and agony of her early days. Through the confidential talks of the two a serenity and calmness came to Lillian. Relief was written on the face of the child. Results were shown in her work. At the time she did some very fine original compositions in music and in her school work she made a real effort to catch up with her class.

In order that the task of completing work might not cause too great discouragement it was advised that Lillian devote her time to making up English and science only. Mathematics and Latin were dropped.

The following year she repeated her mathematics and Latin and took two sophomore subjects. Although she never became an eager student nor entered to a great extent into school life, with exception of athletics, she completed high school with average accomplishment. Emotionally she seemed stable. Because of her talent and interest in music she did not enter college after high school but continued work in music and harmony. She now has musical compositions of real merit to her credit.

Lillian is now happily married and is the mother of

two contented, active youngsters. She gives every evidence of stability and adjustment and is called by her friends, "a charming, well-poised hostess and an understanding mother."

CHAPTER IX

ENVIRONMENTAL PRESSURE: THE CASE OF ALICE WARREN

ALICE WARREN was a member of the junior class in a large public high school. She was sent to the personnel office one day by the principal with the statement that Alice had decided to leave school again, and he had asked her to talk over the whole matter before she left permanently.

Alice appeared with mouth set in a straight line, eyes defiant and an attitude that bespoke revolt. Otherwise, she was a sixteen-year-old girl of attractive appearance, neat and dainty of dress, a form slender and graceful, and a general air of charm. Her mood was indicated by her immediate announcement that it wouldn't do any good to talk to her or to attempt to change her mind for she had decided to quit.

INVESTIGATION OF PRESENT SCHOOL LIFE

Inquiry as to Alice's school work brought the following reports from her teachers:

Bookkeeping.—Alice is the outstanding student in neatness, accuracy, and thinking things out to a logical conclusion. In fact, she goes along quite independently. She has been a model student in my class. Her interest in the work seems high. I can think of no weak points in her as a student or in conduct as she has appeared in my class.

166

English.—I find that Alice does her work for me neatly, intelligently, thoroughly. She is always eager to do her best and if there is anything unusual or lacking in her work she is eager to make proper corrections. Her grades 90, 90, 94 testify to my estimation of the quality of her work. Recently she chose *Romola* for a book review and did an excellent bit of work. Without suggestion from me she drew an interesting comparison with *Macbeth*.

She is shy, seldom volunteering in class although she always knows when she is called upon for discussion and is in the habit of giving more thoughtful and intelligent responses than most of the class. She has not yet read widely of the best literature but I am hoping that she will. I am wondering if she isn't quite introspective. This is merely supposition on my part but a girl with a good mind and yet expresses herself so sparingly, must use that mind on something and it is apt to be herself, is it not?

Typewriting.—Alice's strong points follow: (1) very neat and clean in appearance; (2) always polite and ladylike; (3) seems more interested in her work now than she did at the beginning of the semester; (4) always on time to class and quite regular in attendance. Her weak points: (1) she refuses to hurry; (2) she seems rather stubborn in making up work and in doing class work on time.

Stenography.—Alice is failing in her shorthand. She could do very good work but she never really puts all of her energy into the work. As far as I can see she never shows enthusiasm about anything. Her conduct is always satisfactory but she lacks determination and does not push herself.

Head of Commercial Department.—Alice has very definite strong points: (1) a very good mind, learns easily; (2) proud, wants to be first, and have the best; (3) very neat; (4) works very hard when interested; (5) very close mouthed; (6) has been above board in everything. Weaknesses: (1) she tends to be stubborn; (2) she will not work if she is not interested; (3) she is not reasonable in her desires; (4) she is selfish in the sense that she is so much interested in herself that she does not see the point of view of others.

Tests

Mental Tests.—Alice took the National Intelligence Test and the Terman Group Tests, making the following scores:

ANALYSIS OF NATIONAL INTELLIGENCE TEST

Test	Number Correct	Number Wrong	Score	Possible Score
Computation	21	1	42	44
Information	35	3	35	40
Vocabulary	38	2	36	40
Analogies	28	2	28	32
Comparison	38	0	38	50
TOTAL	160	8	179	206

The conclusion is readily drawn that a ratio of 160 correct to 8 incorrect answers indicates high mental ability.

ANALYSIS OF TERMAN GROUP TESTS OF MENTAL ABILITY

Test	Number Correct	Number Wrong	Score	Possible Score
Information	13	2	13	20
Best Answer	9	2	18	22
Word Meaning	23	4	19	30
Logical Selection	13	7	13	20
Arithmetic	11	1	22	24
Sentence Meaning	18	3	15	24
Analogies	15	3	15	20
Mixed Sentences	15	2	13	18
Classification	15	2	15	18
Number Series	9	3	18	24
TOTAL	141	29	161	220

Score 161 in the Terman test gives a mental age of 17 years and 2 months, which indicates that Alice is advanced 6 months beyond her real age of 16 years and 8 months. Her I.Q. is 128.

By this test Alice's weakest points are logical selection, with 7 wrongs and 13 rights, and number series, with 3 wrongs and 9 rights.

Reading Test.—In the Haggerty Reading Test Alice scored 105. The norm for her grade—XI—is 112; the age norm, 98. The analysis of her results reads:

Test	Number Correct	Number Wrong	Score	Maximum
Vocabulary	39	6	39	50
Sentence Meaning	34	4	30	40
Paragraph	18	9	36	54
TOTAL	91	19	105	144

Character of errors:
  a. Vocabulary

Test Words	Alice's Answers	Test Words	Alice's Answers
parliament	"foreigners"	epaulets	"apparel"
pallid	"darkness"	chalice	"a vase"
revive	"return"	sagacious	"lacking in judgment"

  b. Sentence Meaning
        "Armed cruisers are not vessels of war."
        "Arsenals are primarily for civic meetings."
        "Stalactites are parts of dwellings."
        "Insidious people are not usually deceptive."
  c. Paragraph Meaning
        A long paragraph on knights in combat received three wrong checks out of four, asking for false statements.

Alice's reading apparently had not been of the widest variety, judging from the vocabulary and sentence errors and her difficulty in a quick grasp of tournament rules in knighthood days. Her silent reading was accurate and rapid, and her general understanding good.

Inasmuch as Alice's score on the units in arithmetic in both intelligence tests was so high, the regular arithmetic test was omitted.

In all the tests Alice showed thorough mastery of the mechanics of reading. Her power of analysis, comparison and classification was strong. In writing the tests she worked rapidly, surely, without nervousness and in two instances in the National Test, she completed the test before "stop" was called.

Present Physical Condition.

The report of Alice's physical examination shows her to be in excellent general condition. She is five feet five inches tall and weighs 115 pounds. Her hearing, eyesight, heart and lungs are all described as excellent.

Social Record in School

Alice had no social life in school. She had never joined a club and had never taken part in athletics. Permission to take gymnasium work of any kind had been refused— by her father because he was opposed to the wearing of gymnasium bloomers, "indecent dress," he called them. Her friendships among her classmates were limited to the formal contacts of the classroom.

Mrs. Warren's Version of the Difficulty

In conference with the mother she admitted that she did not understand Alice, who was like her father; she had lived with him for eighteen years now and still did

COMPOSITE PERSONALITY ESTIMATE OF FIVE TEACHERS

	High		Medium		Low	
Refined		x				Coarse
Modest					x	Proud
Cheery			x			Peevish
Courteous		x				Discourteous
Friendly				x		Reserved
Sociable			x			Unsociable
Imaginative	x					Prosaic
Coöperative				x		Combative
Contented					x	Dissatisfied
Optimistic					x	Pessimistic
Keenly alive			x			Apathetic
Loquacious					x	Taciturn
Self-poised	x					Flighty
Common-sense			x			Lacking in judgment
Frank		x				Underhanded
Honest		x				Dishonest
Reliable			x			Unreliable
Prompt			x			Dilatory
Industrious			x			Idle
Attentive			x			Inattentive
Steady			x			Intermittent
Reasonable					x	Unreasonable

not understand him, that he was very "set in his ways."
Alice was just like him. Alice was very proud and
wanted to hold her head up with "the best of 'em." They
couldn't afford to buy her the clothes she wanted, and in
the mother's mind Alice was leaving school because she
wanted *things*. The parents were anxious that Alice complete her high school course and get a good job. All last
summer and since then, there had been no living with her
—always wanted to be on the go, have this, have that,
never wanted to stay at home, seemed ashamed of her

home and of them. Never wanted to go on the street with them any more, always talking about quitting school, never wanted her little sister to go with her.

Of late she had made friends with a young man who drank, went to road houses and ran with fast women, and the parents were much worried that Alice would perhaps get beyond their control and become like the girl next door.

Alice's Version of the Difficulty

During the conference Alice was repeatedly in tears and always utterly hopeless as to the future. When told that all her work was of good quality except stenography and she could easily make that up if she tried, Alice stated that she didn't like it and couldn't do a thing she didn't like to do. Every argument as to her future need of stenography and the necessity in life of doing well the uninteresting and disagreeable task met a set mouth and the same answer, "I can't do it if I don't like it. I don't know why." When asked what she planned to do when she left school, she answered that she did not know, anything so long as she could earn money for herself, have some clothes and do some of the things other girls did to have a good time. She complained that she never was allowed to go anywhere without taking her "kid" sister in the day time and she was not permitted to go out at all at night.

Her parents had always lived in small out-of-the-way places, never had had much schooling, and thought Alice should grow up with the same ideas that they had. She had never had a cent of money which she could call her own. The younger sister was always with her to spy on her movements and to report everything she did to her mother and father. She couldn't stand it any longer— school or anything else. She had made up her mind to quit, if the worst came, she could always kill herself because she did not hold any belief in God or religion anyhow.

Interpretation

This is a conduct case which is just commencing to be a learning case. There is evidence of superior mental ability and adequate previous training. Friction between the mother and Alice as to proper conduct has made Alice the victim of the suspicious spying of the sister. A proud, reticent, self-centered spirit, thwarted on every hand, has brought the thoughts and threats of suicide as the only way out. "I can't if I don't like it" shows a definite volitional inhibition.

INVESTIGATION OF LIFE OUTSIDE OF SCHOOL

The home was the scene of constant quarreling between the father and mother. Mr. Warren was a big, strapping fellow, heavy mustache, black hair, peculiar slant of the eye, a bulldog jaw, and the uncouth appearance of the ordinary working type. In the evening he usually sat before the radio, the one luxury of the home, in his shirt sleeves and bedroom slippers. He appeared calm and courteous. He had always supported his family on day wages. This had required the strictest economy and was the reason why the family lived in a small four-room flat among undesirable neighbors.

Mrs. Warren was of a very excitable nature, "went

all to pieces" and was entirely without refinement or charm. There were no books, papers, magazines, or other marks of taste or culture present. The only sign of cultural improvement was the fact that the younger daughter was being given the opportunity of taking violin lessons.

EARLY HISTORY AND DEVELOPMENT

Family History

Alice's family history was one of poverty in its extreme sense. Even back in the lives of the grandparents on both sides there had been constant deprivation, hard work, and a struggle to make ends meet. They had always lived on a farm, seldom going anywhere week in and week out. A big treat had been an occasional trip to a small town ten miles away.

Mr. and Mrs. Warren had come from the southern part of the middle states where necessities had been luxuries. In these surroundings there had been little beauty and culture. There had been rigid adherence to religious doctrine and form. It was reported that the maternal grandmother had been deeply religious. This had engendered a narrowness of view, a fear of the big outside group, and a tenacity of faith in their own ideas which almost prohibited real coöperation on their part. Both parents had a meager education, having completed the country school course only.

Mr. Warren had been a harness maker. The decreased demand for harnesses had made a steady job difficult to secure. His own account of his boyhood indicated a youngster with a roving, restless nature, headstrong, and with uncontrolled temper. At fifteen he had run away from home; but after five years, his brother had had to pay his fare back home because he could not make a living.

The marriage of Mr. and Mrs. Warren had been necessitated by the pregnancy of the mother. The father, eight years older than the mother, had been twenty-six at the time of his marriage and he had been reaping the harvest of "wild oats" in a very severe case of syphilis. This disease had been contracted by the mother. The result had been the loss of the bridge in her nose. Mrs. Warren had always been, and still is, jealous of her husband. It is exceedingly irritating to her that he is still handsome at forty-two and works in a shop where women are employed.

During the early years of Alice's life, the poverty of her parents had been the deciding factor in the selection of a home and a school. Alice's playmates and associates had been from the very poorest class and, at times, from the most vicious element of society. As a child she had entered the life of this group naturally and normally and had enjoyed the customary sports of childhood, skating, swimming, and other activities with all of her companions.

Physical History

Alice was the oldest of five children. One sister, six years younger, was the only one to survive of the other four. The mother and father were very reticent regarding the details of the past. They talked in general terms only. Any particular question received an indefinite answer.

Emotional History

Alice's advent into this world had not been under auspicious circumstances. At eighteen Mrs. Warren was an expectant mother, morbid and disgraced, both at home and in the community. Her parents with their narrow view of life and living in a world limited by the confines of the immediate neighborhood had been bowed to earth with the shame of their wayward daughter. For many months, Mrs. Warren lived in emotional turmoil. Without doubt her unsettled emotional state had a direct bearing on the mother's attitude toward the new baby. There has been every indication that from the very beginning the unwanted child had been a constant reminder of her disgrace and also a source of irritation. The result had been that there had never existed any understanding or sympathy between Alice and her mother. She had been reared in an atmosphere of jealousy and suspicion especially conducive to emotional upset.

Alice's statement, "I can't do what I don't like to do," must have its foundation in early life. When asked to search her mind for the cause and the earliest recollections of the feeling, Alice told the following enlightening story:

"When I was little, I always got my own way. If denied anything, I planned, lied, and persisted, until I won out. I have always done so. What I want, I get—what I don't want, I won't have. I *am* like my father. He has always been restless. When he has lived in one place for a time he packs up and moves to another. When I was about two years old my father got the promise of a job in another town and turned in his time at the place where he was working. For some reason he failed to get the work he had been promised, and he was too proud to go to his boss and ask for his old job back again, so he moved to a new place. When he got settled he had only forty-five cents left. He hunted for work everywhere but could find none. He was out of a job for seven months and we almost starved. Because they had to, my folks began to pick up things they needed, such as food and articles of clothing, at the ten-cent store and wherever else they could.

"When my father finally got a job he still picked up things that came handy. The first thing I ever picked up was a skein of embroidery silk in the first grade. From that time until two years ago, I have picked up things I wanted most, bits of jewelry from the ten-cent store and knick-knacks, and spent my money for the big things. The last thing I took was this watch, two years ago, and I made up my mind then that I'd never take another thing, and I haven't."

Asked as to her own attitude about *stealing*, for she had constantly used the term "picked up," Alice said she had never felt a twinge of conscience, that church people were hypocrites, and it was a case of "crook outwit a crook," and get what you can; that she didn't believe in God so there was no question of right and wrong in her life.

Alice was aware of the condition of her mother and lately had felt fear and shame lest she be the victim of the same disease. One day she was absent from school because her face was all broken out in an infected mass. To the school, this seemed to be the opportune time to settle the question as to whether Alice had been infected with syphilis or not. At first, when it was suggested to Alice that she go to a physician about her skin difficulty, she was hesitant, being uncertain as to her inheritance. Furthermore, her mother opposed it most decidedly. Alice, however, wanted to go to work in an office, so her office work was used as a leverage on her mother, and finally her reluctant consent was given. A blood test was made and samples sent to the state health department without the knowledge of Alice and Mrs. Warren. The examination was paid for by one of the instructors interested in Alice's development. The result of the test was negative. When Alice was told that she had a very simple skin eruption which would be gone in a couple of days, her mind was greatly relieved. A few days later she said, "Look at me! I have nothing to fear. I'm a specimen of perfect health."

Alice lived in an atmosphere of friction. Mrs. Warren was constantly telling her that she would come to some bad end. In fact, she strongly resembled her cousin who had kept bad companions and turned out to be wayward. So bad had been the cousin that her father had committed suicide when she could not be brought back into the fold of decency.

School History

Alice's school history had been one of many changes, eighteen in number, as she had moved from place to place, the victim of the changing fortune of her parents. No records were available for this period.

Alice entered the first year of high school from another state. Her grades for various studies in high school have been:

First Semester		*Second Semester*	
English	91	English 2	91
Algebra	94	Algebra 2	96
Physiology	91	Business Training	91
Foods	90	Foods	C

Third Semester		*Fourth Semester*	
English 3	96	English 4	92
Geography	91	Latin	91
Commercial Arithmetic.	94	Geography 2	92
Bookkeeping	94	Commercial Arithmetic 2	94
		Bookkeeping	94

Fifth Semester	
English 5	90
Bookkeeping 3	93
Typing 1	78
Stenography	F

Interpretation

In Alice's developmental history these facts seem significant:

1. Alice has been totally without moral training by precept or example on the part of the home.

2. The hypocrisy of her parents, who had been deeply religious by profession but without even moral principle in practice, distorted Alice's ideas of people in general. Her glib quotation of antisocial remarks showed the nature of the parental attitude.

3. A complete absence of refinement in the home and parents was felt and resented by Alice as she made the comparisons through school contacts. "My folks are determined that I shall be just as they are, and I won't do it."

4. A decided egoism has been developed in Alice through lack of restraint or guidance.

5. Alice's inherited tendencies have been magnified by the

uncontrolled temper of the father and the hysterical excitability of the mother.

6. A restlessness shown by the family history is reflected in Alice's school work. She worked for a time, then suddenly wanted to break the monotony by dropping out of school altogether.

DIAGNOSIS

Primary, Causation.—There has been an emotional conflict from earliest childhood caused by a strong will exerting itself in self-satisfaction at any cost, due to the absolute and continuous lack of satisfaction of normal desires because of poverty.

Secondary Causation.—There consequently developed the volitional inhibition: "I can't if I don't like it."

Tertiary Causation.—In childhood, the above conflict created an antisocial attitude resulting in stealing and lying; in adolescence, it produced a feeling of shame of parents and home.

Contributory Causation.—Contributory causes were emotional and environmental:

a. Conception and birth under conditions of emotional stress
b. Poverty and poor home influence, with its religious hypocrisy, suspicion, and direct training in stealing
c. Poor neighborhood contacts and standards
d. Fear of disease and the resemblance to the wayward cousin
e. Hereditary tendency to restlessness, love of change, and resistance to tasks involving any sort of monotony
f. A very superior intelligence which caused Alice to be alert to differences in social and economic levels, and made her dissatisfied with her lot

Support of Diagnosis

At the age of two years, the most impressionable period in life, Alice went through the experience of actual hunger and cold. Food and fuel could not be provided by the home unless secured by dishonest means. The normal childish craving for little toys, playthings, pretty ornaments and knick-knacks, was constantly unsatisfied. Hand in hand with this normal craving went a will-power that would gain satisfaction at any price. Whatever Alice wanted, that Alice had. Thus the inimical conflict was established. From this developed the volitional inhibition, "I can't if I don't like it," which is merely the negative form of "I want it and I am going to have it," a characteristic of Alice from babyhood.

The practice of stealing begun by the parents by seeming necessity, was continued as an easy means of satisfying their wants, so that Alice, without any training in word or example as to the rights of personal property, took a skein of bright-colored embroidery silk to satisfy her craving for pretty things. According to her own statement, as she used the silk to outline the pictures on cards, she felt no pang of conscience nor any sense of guilt. What she had learned was that if things were taken one must not be caught. To be detected was to do wrong. Being unusually bright and alert, Alice had not been found out; therefore, in her mind, she was not guilty. Alice positively asserted that never had the act of "picking up" things been accompanied by a feeling of guilt. As is well known, morals must be taught and be acquired through training, so her statement is no doubt true. From the fact that no article had been taken which did not, at the time, seem a necessity in satisfying a desire for ornament, dress, or object of play, it is conceivable that had Alice's parents been willing and financially able to satisfy her desire for *normal* wants, there would have been no history of stealing on her part.

In adolescence there came a change in Alice. Due to associations in high school and to a perfectly wholesome and normal interest in boys, the unfulfilled longing for natural desires led to a feeling of shame of her home and her parents. She realized that she was bright and attractive and there was no reason why she should not have the same things and enjoy the same pleasures as the other girls whom she saw every day. To satisfy her wants, she was determined to quit school and to earn money to buy things for herself. If necessary she would commit suicide and end the craving altogether.

Furthermore, her strong will became an inhibiting force whenever Alice was confronted with a task she did not want to do. She was failing in stenography. This involved the monotony of endless repetition. Having inherited a restless spirit and encouraged by the constant changes brought about in eighteen different schools, it is no wonder that she rebelled at the monotonous tasks and entertained the thought of satisfying her own desires by quitting school.

Alice was a bundle of emotions. Born under the influence of the emotional agony of a mother who had incurred the anger of her own parents and the scorn of her neighbors, growing from girlhood into womanhood under the dread secret of a diseased father and mother, fearful that she too might become a victim, constantly reminded that she resembled the wayward cousin, Alice lived in a maelstrom of emotions. To aggravate the whole emotional upset, in the developing stages of sex instinct, the home surrounded her with an atmosphere of suspicion and a cruel, galling spy system. The result was inner rebellion and emotional instability.

Certain other very definite factors were also operating as influences upon Alice. Her tendency to satisfy her wishes in any way possible and with no consideration for the interests of others was encouraged by the fact that her parents ignored the rights of others and that they had taught her to do the same. How could they now expect consideration from her? Her playmates and the unwritten law of the locality in which she lived offered no reproof of her acts in terms of higher ideals. She did not possess the restraint of a belief in God as One who sees and cares for the individual. Finally, if she had been of more sluggish mentality there would probably have been less emotional conflict. Things would have been accepted as she found them and she would have had little desire to better herself and her conditions. Her superior mentality made it impossible for her to be satisfied with the plane of living with which her parents were apparently contented. She said, "They want me to be like them and I will not."

TREATMENT

When Alice had been persuaded to stay in school a little longer, at least until she could graduate, a few remedial measures were started at once. A change in her program was made to provide the teacher personality Alice seemed to need. Normal school activities were commenced. Alice was put into a gymnasium class, the school providing the uniform. Arrangements were also made for her to attend the Home Economics Club.

Two weeks slipped by and one afternoon Alice unexpectedly appeared after school and asked for an interview. When alone she begged for suggestions as to ways to make money, saying she would be willing to do housework on Saturdays or anything that could be found in order to have a little spending money of her own; that now the only way she could go to shows was with a young man who was "wild" and she'd like to be able to go with a girl friend occasionally.

Through the head of the commercial department work was secured for Alice in an office after school and on Saturdays. It was thought that the first remedial step must be to give Alice an opportunity for things other people enjoyed. As fast as the weekly salary came into her hands she began to get the pretty necessities she had wanted. In order that the period of waiting for gratification might not be too long and that the most needed items might be secured rather soon, through an arrangement with department store heads, articles of wearing apparel were reduced in price to meet Alice's limited resources, and the balance paid by those interested in her welfare. Every effort was made, however, so that this was not carried to the extreme. Everything seemed to be going very well.

One morning Alice came to the worker's office with the request for another interview. She was going to leave home; she couldn't stand it any longer; every minute she spent at home was used in argument as to where she had been, why she didn't get home earlier, why she went to school so early; the "kid" sister was sent everywhere with her again; her father had thrashed her with a razor strop, hard, too, because she had been saucy; that morning when she started for school earlier than her mother approved of, she had been promised another thrashing when she came home at noon; her father was planning to put her in the Home for Delinquent Girls so she could not meet her young man; he was threatening to take her wages away from her so she could not be independent; so, she wasn't going home to be thrashed. This story came out with the tears rolling down Alice's face. There was no hysteria, just a dead white face with the old desperate look—and tears.

Alice was reassured that she need not be frightened by threats of the Home for Delinquent Girls swallowing her at some unexpected moment, since court action would be necessary; that in these days a sixteen-year-old girl need not submit to repeated thrashings by her parents, and that provision would be made for her outside the home if things did not change. Alice was sent to the rest room. In the meantime, the mother had called the principal to inquire if Alice was in school. She stated that she had been going early to school and it might be merely an excuse to meet the "wild" young man. This message was used by the case-worker as a pretext to call at the home.

In half an hour the mother had confirmed everything that Alice had said, with additional information that proved continuous suspicion: spying by opening Alice's letters, both those sent and those received, arrangements for Alice's being watched by certain high-school girls, while she was at school, the discussion of Alice's being placed in the Home for Delinquent Girls, and a visit to the probation officer for that purpose.

The mother was told kindly and plainly that in these days parents are not permitted to thrash sixteen-year-old girls, that the Court would not permit a nice girl like Alice to be sent to a reformatory, that their treatment of Alice was inhuman in its suspicion and spy system and could end in one of two ways, suicide as she had threatened or an elopement with the undesirable young man. Assurance was given as to Alice's exemplary conduct at school, the respect of her teachers, and the fine type of work of which she was capable if she could only have a happy home life.

Later, in answer to questions as to the suspicions of her mother, Alice assured the case-worker that she had not seen, written to, or talked with the young man for over two weeks, that she had never known sex experience although she had petted. At this time she was shown the close relation between petting, the sex act, and childbirth, and the reason for that relation and the danger involved when step one was taken and step two had to be inhibited. Alice always explained her parents' attitude of suspicion toward her by the fact that she resembled closely her wayward cousin.

The weeks slipped by until they were nine in number. Alice had appeared in a new outfit, a coat, a school dress, shoes and hat, purchased from her own earnings. Her school work in the second semester was well under way, with one subject, economics, under the instruction of the case-worker. In this way an opportunity was afforded for a close observation of her reactions in the classroom. She appeared perfectly normal, interested in the boys about her but not too much so, volunteering, answering questions, and seemingly with a keen interest in the subject matter and the group. She was somewhat timid in taking the lead in class discussions but gave evidence of thorough preparation when called upon. She had a bright, vivacious face, alight with interest.

One afternoon, at the opening of class hour, Alice walked directly to the desk and said abruptly, "I had a quarrel with my father this noon over quitting school and he told me to pack my clothes and get out. Where shall I go?" Where, indeed, with only forty-five minutes remaining between the close of the class hour and the time when Alice was due at her place of work. It was suggested that her father was angry and did not mean what he had said, but Alice replied, "Now is my chance and I'm going to take it."

Through the influence of a friend, a happily married young woman, a graduate nurse and the mother of two little girls, four and six years of age, was persuaded to take Alice into her home. She lived in a new bungalow, a mile from Alice's home, in a good neighborhood. She was herself of a cheery disposition with a sane, wholesome view of life. It was felt that the whole atmosphere of the house would be in strong contrast to that from which Alice had come and would give her an opportunity for a new start if she sincerely wished one.

A visit to Alice's home next morning was illuminating. Mrs. Warren was in a high state of excitement in which her main thought seemed to be to justify herself and blame her daughter. The story seemed to be that Alice had goaded her father the day before until he had ordered her out of the house; she (the mother) had been so nervous all the afternoon that when the ambulance came toward the house she had nearly fainted for she thought Alice might have committed suicide.   Mrs. Warren declared that somebody had been putting independent ideas into Alice's head lately and "she couldn't do nothing with her any more."

That evening a second visit was made to the home to see the father, with the hope that this home might be brought into coöperation with the school and in some way these two agencies might solve its difficulties together. Mr. Warren went over the events that had led to Alice's leaving home, blaming the girl for being unmanageable, although he did admit that he should not have lost his temper as badly as he had.   Dogmatically he asserted that now that she was gone, however, she could learn her lesson; that he would not ask her to come back but that she was welcome any time she wanted to come; that he had sent his wife down town to finish paying for Alice's coat which she was buying on installments, so that she could have her wages of five-fifty a week for her own needs.   He confided to the case-worker that he, too, had run away from home when he was fifteen.   He said he had never known of a school before that took so much interest in its pupils, by getting them jobs, keeping them in school, and trying to improve their conditions.   When the conference closed it appeared that the parents were reconciled to the experiment, and if they were not exactly pleased, still they would not interfere with Alice's plans.

Five days later, at eight-thirty in the evening, Alice came to the worker's home in an excited state, her face like chalk.   She had gone home for the rest of her clothes and when her father asked about her new home, she had told him how lovely and pleasant it was and how very happy and contented she felt. At the statement he had become very angry that she was not ready to bow to his wishes and to come home; he had refused to allow her to take her clothes; he had given her one day in which to return home or he'd send a policeman after her. He said that he had been talking to some men about the whole affair and they said that he could make his daughter mind until she was eighteen years old, that the woman where the girl was staying had made herself liable to arrest by "coaxing her away from home," that his child should be forced to come back home and behave herself. Thoroughly scared by the threats, Alice had come to give warning to her benefactors.

One day elapsed. The next morning the probation officer appeared at the principal's office with an order from the state's attorney to return the girl to her home.

Fortunately the probation officer had visited the home first. There her process of enlightenment had begun and had grown rapidly. "Mrs. Warren," she said, "had presented the case to the state's attorney as that of a wayward girl whom the parents could no longer control, stating that she had been coaxed away from the home and from the protection of her parents who had in vain tried to keep her in nights; that one night she had been out until one o'clock (the mother did not say that the little sister was with her), and that now Mrs. Warren was appealing to the law for help." The state's attorney, naturally impulsive and headstrong and given to snap judgments, was ready to play the hero part and come to the rescue; he had called the probation officer and sent her out to take care of the matter. She had learned from

the mother that the day before she herself had gone to
all the drug stores in town and had warned them not to
sell poison to her daughter, then she had warned the
police to be on the look-out for her because a woman at
the high school and another woman with whom Alice was
living had coaxed the girl away from her mother. Mrs.
Warren was determined to bring Alice back even if she
did commit suicide; she'd rather put her in the Home
for Delinquent Girls than leave her in the house where
she was; she was going to take her wages away from her
and show her she had to mind her mother and behave herself. The officer went on to say that the attitude of the
mother was so unreasonable and so evidently actuated by
jealousy that she remonstrated with her, telling her she
should think of the girl's welfare and not her own wishes.
To this the mother replied, "Well, I see you and I can't get
together on this," and the officer said, "No, we can't,
for you are not showing any love for your daughter. You
are only jealous that she can be happy outside of the
home."

After a conference at the school, the officer assured
the school that she was on the girl's side and would go to
the state's attorney with her report and that her decision
would be that the girl should not be returned to her home
without a trial.

A conference was arranged between the principal and
Mr. Warren in the presence of the latter's employer. At
the time the father was shown frankly how his home and
family had fallen down on its job. Mr. Warren came to
the decision that he would let the matter rest and give
Alice an opportunity to continue her experiment of living outside the home.

That night the mother had a long fainting spell, seemed out of her head, kept moaning and lamenting that the school had taken her daughter away from her and that Alice did not love her any more. So a physician was summoned. A policeman came for Alice, the father accompanying him, telling her kindly he would take her to see her mother and bring her back again immediately, if she cared to return. Alice went and found the bed surrounded by women from the neighboring apartments who began to upbraid her. To these she replied, "You don't know anything about it."

The next morning Alice came to school looking so white and ill that she was kept out of classes and allowed to spend the morning in the rest room. Later she went to see her mother in the company of the probation officer. When she returned she said that she did not care to go home any more, it only made things worse and she could never go back to become what her mother was. "My father will never go to court. I know too much about him. He hasn't been moving from place to place all these years without good reason."

A week-end was planned for Alice which would give her a rest and a change of environment. Saturday was spent in Chicago, where she had never been. She visited the Chapel at the University, Field Museum, the Public Library, and Marshall Field's. Alice was happy and enthusiastic. Sunday, too, was spent with a friend in her home.

Alice arrived on Sunday in good spirits, her face animated and interested, her appearance neat and attractive. The three, Alice, her hostess, and Frances, the daughter, chatted about things in general, the trip to Chicago,

Alice's new Easter outfit, books, movies, and church. But it was Alice's Easter outfit that drew the friend's attention. The shoes were to be red, in fact she had bought them the day before. They had taken all of her week's salary ($5.50). The stockings were to be light tan, the dress red, and the hat and gloves tan. Alice's face, voice and manner were a revelation. She was aglow, her eyes sparkling with anticipation, her whole heart centered on the fulfillment of her desires. She had planned to make the hat from one given to her by the lady with whom she lived, the dress was to be bought from the next week's salary ($5.50) and then when everything was ready, on Easter day, she was going to walk up and down the streets so people could see her in her new outfit!

A nephew of the friend called in the afternoon. Alice's reaction was a perfectly natural one. She became more quiet in her tones, talked less, but was perfectly at ease; she knew she looked just right in her neat "dollar-day" dress, and her manner showed it. She talked easily and in animation on her own level. So far her reading choice had been in light romance and mystery stories, her musical taste in jazz, and her personal ambition pretty clothes and handsome young men—in all she seemed a perfectly normal adolescent girl, without any cultural background.

When she went away there was a spirit of friendliness that she had not shown before that seemed to say, "I understand it all now. There is a difference."

The very next morning Alice came to the office asking again that she might drop typing, using the same excuse she had given before in dropping stenography, "I don't like it and I can't do it." This time, however, the worker looked directly into Alice's eyes for a minute and said seriously, "Alice, this feeling that you can't do what you don't like to do is very serious. You can never succeed in anything until you find out why you feel that way and try to overcome it. Furthermore, no one else can help you, either."

Alice thought seriously for a few minutes and said, "I believe that the whole difficulty is connected with my early life. The principle in my family has always been 'Get what you can in any way you can. Don't get caught.' If things were not to my liking, I did something to change them. Nobody ever made me mind. If I didn't want to do something, I just didn't do it. Lying and stealing mean nothing to me. I don't believe in God."

"Alice, would you trust your friend if you knew that she lied whenever it was to her advantage to do so, that she refused to do things just because she didn't want to do them, that in the stores she stole whenever she wanted to satisfy a desire?"

"No, of course I wouldn't. I told you this because I knew you would understand."

"Well, don't you see that there must be some people in the world whom other people can trust, in order to carry on the work of the world? What is to become of the little child that sometime must look to you for advice and help, if she can't trust you and know that you are true?"

"I'm never going to get married. There will never be any child of mine."

"That won't change the situation. There will always be those who must depend upon your trustworthiness—even now, at the office where you work they must trust you—the school must trust you now to do the fair thing where you are living. How can you be put into the home of a friend if you cannot be trusted?"

"Oh, but you can. I wouldn't think of taking anything from people I knew."

"But don't you see, Alice, it is our ideas of right and wrong that make us the *kind* of people that *can* be trusted? Right and wrong are standards set up by society so that we can live together. Our idea of God helps to make those standards—gives us a plumb line. Suppose you had never seen an electric light bulb and I tried to tell you of the unseen power inside, and you said, 'I don't believe it,' would that change the truth at all, or would it just be tragic that you did not *believe* the truth?"

"I see," said Alice.

The next morning she came in and announced that she had decided to continue with her typing. This decision was evidence of beginning growth.

Jeannette, a lovely, wholesome girl in the senior class, with an understanding, cultured mother, was taken into the plan of reconstruction enough to become interested in Alice. She was changed into Alice's gymnasium class where gradually she worked up an acquaintanceship. It was not an easy matter, for Alice held aloof for a long time, giving way only little by little to the friendly, casual advances of a new friend. Finally an invitation to dinner was accepted by Alice. She was all excited and burst into the office saying, "Jeannette is going to teach me how to dance. She and her young man took me home from school last night and I took them in and introduced them to Mrs. Brown, my foster mother. Jeannette has invited me to her house for dinner. I shall never go with

Gordon (the wild young man) again. There are three nice boys in school I'd like to go with now that I have a home to take them into. You know I couldn't ask anybody decent into my folks' home. They'd never have come a second time." It was not until Alice had moved to her foster home that it was realized how fully she had been controlled by shame of her home and its environment. In talking over the whole situation, Alice said, "You know I just *had* to get away soon. I could never be any different there and I want to be different. Now I can live my own life and be friends with the family at the same time."

At the dinner she was initiated into the joys of dancing, and had such a good time that there was no longer a question as to the friendship becoming established. Jeannette had in mind the inclusion of other girls of Alice's own junior class and some boy friends, so that by the close of the school year Alice might have her own social group. Her foster home was open to her friends and Mrs. Brown took an interest in all her affairs.

Shortly after the dinner party, Alice came in and asked if she might try out for a junior play. This step, taken on her own initiative, showed that the reconstruction process within herself had already begun. She was given a part in the play—small indeed—but it made her feel an integral part of the social group.

The settlement in a happy, congenial family, where she worked for her board and room, made possible two helpful influences: that of a harmonious atmosphere, and the necessity for filling a place of responsibility in a family group by having certain duties to perform regularly and well. Alice had never been given any responsibility in her own home nor had she ever been taught how to perform any household duties.

The effect of emotional calm was at once evident in Alice's reactions. She went about the house singing, joined in the fun and laughter of the children, and began to sleep so soundly that no noise, however unusual, could awaken her.

For three months everything went very well. One evening Alice's mother invited her to her birthday dinner. Alice returned home for the occasion. A few days later she came to the worker with the question of going home permanently saying that her mother had offered every inducement. All points of former contention were to be yielded. Alice was not to be forced to go to school any more, she was to be permitted to spend her money as she pleased and to go whenever and wherever she chose.

This created a difficult situation. Recently Alice had begun to show a reluctance to assume responsibility in household duties in her foster home. Was the opportunity to return home desired merely to avoid meeting obligations? Were Alice advised to remain in her new home the mother would seem justified in her contention that the school had taken Alice away from her; on the other hand, to advise Alice to return to the old conditions meant the probable loss of all ground gained. It was made clear to Alice that the decision must rest entirely with her as she had left home of her own free will because she had felt that conditions there were no longer to be borne. Had her absence produced a real need and longing for her home that would prove an incentive in making the best of trying conditions? Had there been a real change in the home attitude which would make possible an understanding between her and her parents? She alone could answer these questions.

Two days later the decision was made. Alice moved back to her own home. Almost immediately there was a change in Alice. The outstanding points were irregular attendance at school with a low grade in typing and the renewal of intimacy with the "wild" young friend. School work suffered.

At the end of the junior year it was necessary for Alice to attend summer school as she had failed in typing. Thereupon new resolutions were made. Dates with young men who were intemperate and unsteady were to be a thing of the past. Again strong determination to study hard and to make honor grades in her senior year came to the fore.

During this time her employment was steady and her desire for pretty clothes and personal adornment seemed to have been satisfied. Now she turned her attention to the home. Through her influence, the family moved into a six-room apartment. New furniture was purchased with Alice's financial aid, touches of refinement were added so that the home was transformed in appearance and atmosphere.

Progress seemed permanent. Steadying qualities appeared in her last year in high school. Her attitude was excellent, her attendance regular and the following high grades were to her credit: home economics, 92; economic society, 87; United States history, 84; office training and salesmanship, 92. She ranked fifteenth in a class of two hundred and eighteen. There was also definite improvement in the family relationship. Although the violent temper of her father resulted in occasional quarrels, Alice was learning self-control and restraint so that she was able to live above the family discord. Alice had regular work on a longer schedule and her pay was increased accordingly.

With graduation from high school Alice passed from the relationship of daily contact with the school to that which was advisory in character and entirely voluntary. The confidence established by two years of friendly interest has held throughout the years following her graduation. The first six months after graduation were difficult and of great significance to Alice. With the freedom of action permitted by her parents and with her economic independence through self-support came varied temptations and experiences of a serious nature. Emotionally she was little prepared for them and at times it appeared as if Alice might not win out in her struggle and might revert to the character of her family. In every case Alice came voluntarily to the school for advice and guidance.

Two years have passed since Alice left the high school. The family has made another move and are now established in a very desirable seven-room house where everything is as Alice has dreamed a home should be. She has a steady position, loves her work and is independent and happy.

A recent incident is evidence of her genuine character development. Involved in a trying situation out of which she could have escaped easily by a simple lie, Alice stood her ground, told the truth and took her penalty. In recounting the incident she declared, "I wouldn't lie about it." What a far cry from the comment which Alice had once made, "If denied anything, I plan, lie and persist until I win out."

Life is a process of adjustment in which the varied experiences of the individual mold his character and determine his personality. Life has been hard on Alice and has put her through a vigorous training. The struggle has not been easy but from it all has emerged a real personality. Egoism has given way to altruism. Through the grilling process she has clung to the finer things of life. Her deliberate choice has been higher ideals, a genuine proof of an adjusted personality.

CHAPTER X

PARENTAL DOMINANCE: THE CASE OF BETTY ROBERTS

BETTY ROBERTS was a freshman who had entered high school from a public elementary school. She was enrolled in science I, English I, mathematics I and elementary design. At the end of the first semester she had failed all subjects.

INVESTIGATION OF PRESENT SCHOOL LIFE

The facts in Betty's case as given in the reports of her instructors may be summed up as follows:

1. She seems to think it unnecessary to help herself, for assistance must be given to her on every detail.
2. She is very immature in her mental outlook.
3. She never responds or shows any reaction to anything that goes on in class.
4. She is apparently poorly prepared.
5. She is not inclined to be teachable.
6. She has a wrong attitude in regard to criticism and is usually inclined to cry or to assume a petulant attitude when she is criticized.
7. When she gives floor talks she is unusually nervous and panicky.
8. She is very aloof and unapproachable.
9. She seems very unhappy.

A study was made of Betty's capacity for application during her mathematics periods for about a month and the observations recorded.

SUSTAINED APPLICATION STUDY UNIT IN MATHEMATICS

Date	Length of Period	Distraction		Application		Per Cent of Application
March 29.	44′	11′	20″	32′	40″	74
30.	43′	29′	30″	13′	30″	31
31.	24′	20′	30″	3′	30″	15
April 1.	45′	20′	50″	19′	10″	43
5.	40′	16′		24′		60
6.	40′	13′	20″	26′	40″	66
7.	40′	12′	40″	27′	20″	68
8.	40′	16′	10″	23′	50″	59
11.	35′	12′	40″	22′	20″	64
13.	45′	11′	40″	33′	20″	74
14.	23′	5′		18′		77
15.	45′	23′	20″	21′	40″	48
18.	45′	26′	30″	18′	30″	41
19.	44′	4′	40″	39′	20″	89
20.	30′	1′	20″	28′	40″	91
TOTAL ..	583	230′	30″	352′	30″	60

Tests

According to the Otis Higher Examination Betty had an I.Q. of 112.

In five other tests she scored as follows:

	Betty's Score	Norms, Grade IX
Inglis Vocabulary Test	68	45
Monroe Silent Reading Test		
Comprehension	39	25.4
Rate	100	84
Thorndike-McCall Reading Scale ...	72	61.5
Reavis-Breslich Diagnostic Test	52	53.75

Present Physical Condition

Betty's weight was normal (119.7 pounds). The condition of her ears and eyes was reported as good. Her pulse on standing was 72; after exercise, 100. She had a slight acne.

Social Record in School

Betty had few friends and entered very little, if any, into the group activities of the school. Even in gymnasium classes she was retiring and extremely self-conscious. Her own classmates said that she could not be drawn into the group because she was so queer and disagreeable.

A composite of instructors' ratings described her as refined, peevish, irritable, reserved, indifferent, sullen, unsociable, taciturn, combative, apathetic, dissatisfied, dilatory and inattentive.

Betty was asked to rate herself. The results are interesting and indicative.

When Betty had finished checking the chart she started to cry and sobbed, "Inside I'm all the good traits, outside I'm all the bad ones."

Parents' Version of the Difficulty

The father's explanation of Betty's poor work was that she did not want to do well and was determined not to adjust to the school at all. She and her mother had conceived the idea that Betty should be sent to a fashionable boarding school. It was *the thing to do*. Mr. Roberts had put his foot down and declared that when he said no, he meant no. In his mind, Betty had always been too reserved, and she never wanted to be shown off to his friends. When the mother was asked if she had any explanation for Betty's difficulty she lightly answered,

BETTY'S PERSONALITY RATING OF HERSELF

Trait	High		Medium		Low	Trait
Refined	x					Coarse
Modest	x					Vain
Democratic			x			Snobbish
Cheery		x				Peevish
Patient		x				Irritable
Courteous		x				Discourteous
Friendly		x				Reserved
Cordial		x				Indifferent
Sociable		x				Unsociable
Imaginative			x			Prosaic
Altruistic			x			Selfish
Coöperative			x			Combative
Open-to-suggestion		x				Opinionated
Contented					x	Dissatisfied
Optimistic					x	Pessimistic
Keenly alive				x		Apathetic
Loquacious				x		Taciturn
Self-poised			x			Flighty
Calm			x			Excitable
Trustful		x				Jealous
Well-spoken		x				Gossipy
Common-sense		x				Lacking in judgment
Frank		x				Underhanded
Honest	x					Dishonest
Reliable	x					Unreliable
Reasonable			x			Unreasonable
Prompt			x			Dilatory
Industrious			x			Idle
Attentive			x			Inattentive
Steady		x				Intermittent

"Oh, she'll be all right if we ever get her away. She is the oldest and she has had to grow up too fast."

Betty's Story

The first conferences with Betty were very unproductive. At one time she sat for fifteen minutes without uttering a sound and answered all questions with a nod of her head. After several interviews she began to show less resentment and grew more talkative. She offered the information that she knew that she could do better but she hated the school, the girls and three of her teachers. Toward the science teacher most of her animosity was directed. He was disliked for no other reason than "that everybody else liked him and he was very popular." It was her earnest desire to be expelled from school. That would bring her father to time, she knew, and she would then be permitted to go away from home. When she was pressed as to her reason for disliking the girls of the school she promptly stated, "They all dislike me. I'd like to be popular and smart, too." "Smart and popular like whom?" was asked. Betty named one of the outstanding senior girls who had been exceptional in social contacts and academic work.

Interpretation

Betty's failure is not due to native inability. All test scores are above the norm for her grade. Her whole difficulty seems to be one of wrong attitude. Instructors and girls characterize her as disagreeable, irritable, reserved, combative and hostile to criticism and correction, and queer. On the other hand, Betty describes herself as cheery, patient, friendly, sociable and open to suggestion; yet she admits that she is dissatisfied and pessimistic. She dislikes the school for no reason except that she wants to be somewhere else. The girls and the instructors are distasteful to her for no plausible reason at all. She does not do the work because she doesn't want to do it. Sixty per cent attention for fifteen days' work can bring success in very few cases. Such an attitude must have its root and origin in something other than plain, human perversity. What is the cause of her half-hearted attention? There must be something working in the background that causes the girl to present to the outside world the wrong picture of herself, when "inside she is all the good traits," as she says. There is evidence of antagonism toward her father. Perhaps the school attitude is merely the reflection of a home situation.

INVESTIGATION OF LIFE OUTSIDE OF SCHOOL

The physical needs of the Roberts family were well taken care of. The meals were well balanced, the children had sufficient sleep and there was a commendable orderliness about the home. There was ample space for the older children to have their own bedrooms, and these rooms were well fitted in every respect for study.

Betty's social life outside of school was as cramped and restrained as her school life. She knew no girls or boys intimately and did nothing in a social or recreational way except to go to a play or a movie with the family.

The members of the household numbered ten; the parents, three boys, three girls and two servants. The atmosphere of the home was decidedly *"nouveau riche."* One felt as if the books, the pictures and the furniture and its very arrangement were not a part of the family. Everything was too perfect and the impression created was that things were bought for appearance's sake, that is, to convince the visitor that the family really belonged to a certain stratum of society. For example, the book shelves were loaded with fine editions of standard works of the best authors but the casual handling of a few volumes showed that they were not read. It was evident that they were practically untouched, stiff and with the pages uncut.

At the time of the first visit Mrs. Roberts was not at home. Although the youngest child was only nine months old the mother had left the whole family in charge of the housekeeper while she spent a month in Biloxi, not because she was ill but because her husband had been very irritable and dictatorial.

Although Betty was the oldest of the family she seemed to assume no more responsibility toward the house and the children than the others. Her whole attitude in the home was negative and passive.

Two penalty cards had been sent to the home by the school stating that Betty was doing very little in science and mathematics. After Betty and the other children had retired, Mr. Roberts explained that he felt very guilty about the feeling he had exhibited when the cards were received in the home. He went on to relate that he had become very, very angry at Betty's poor work and had stormed around the house and "raised hell in general," as he put it. He would not have such work in *his* household. He hadn't climbed to such heights and become so prominent only to be disgraced by a member of *his* family. From now on Betty was to have no privileges of any kind. After these statements he had left the house immediately and he had thought little more about the scene until later in the evening. As he passed Betty's door he stepped into her room because her bedside lamp was still lighted. Betty was sound asleep but pinned to the lamp was a note to her father. It read, "I wish I was dead. Betty."

Interpretation

The home life gives further evidence of disharmony. Because of the irritability of the father Mrs. Roberts had left the city. For the same reason Betty had gone to bed a most unhappy and pessimistic little girl. In the home there is evidence of pretense and an apparent striving to be something one is not.

Early Developmental History

Pregnancy and birth were normal. Walking and talking had started at the proper time. Before Betty was seven she had had whooping-cough, chicken-pox, measles, a tonsillectomy, and an adenoidectomy but no serious consequences had resulted. Most of these diseases of childhood had come in the early years of her school life. The record showed that she had been absent from school very little.

A glimpse into the history of the father is illuminating. Mr. Roberts had been born and raised in the slums of an eastern city, among the "trash of humanity," as he put it. At the age of twelve, through a fine young man in the neighborhood settlement house, his ambition had been fired and he had wanted to get an education and "be somebody." A program of long hours and hard work during the daytime and persistent effort at night school was carried on diligently for years. Correspondence work and more night school and at last a diploma from a law school was gained. He had married after that and Betty was the first child. During the early years of his married life there had been little money, few comforts and a constant struggle to make ends meet. Suddenly politics began to play into Mr. Roberts' hands and almost over night he was thrust from obscurity into the public limelight. Newspapers quoted him and photographed him and in certain sections of the country his name was a household word.

The mother, a pretty young woman, who had had little schooling beyond the eighth grade, had not kept pace with her husband. She read very little, went to few concerts and belonged to few organizations of a cultural character. Her time during the first years of marriage had been well occupied with the numerous babies who had come into the family within a comparatively few years. But there was one respect in which she had kept to the fore: She was always beautifully and fashionably dressed.

Four years previous to Betty's entrance into high school Mrs. Roberts had changed her religion because, as she said, "I was not in harmony with life." At once there had resulted constant bickering and quarreling between husband and wife. It was her boast that when Mr. Roberts became unbearable she packed up her things and left town.

Such is the atmosphere in which Betty was raised. There had been in the early life too little of material things, now there was too much. Earlier there had been a home of peacefulness, now there was discord.

School History

Betty had liked school well enough, and she had had no special difficulty nor any outstanding success. She had been an average student and had always passed. About four years before she had begun to feel unhappy because she thought that she could not do superior work as many did. Next came the idea that girls and boys didn't like her. Betty's philosophy was, "Why should any one work so hard, anyhow? Where did it get you? If you got a high position you just had to keep on working just the same. There was no rest. Push, push, push!" When Betty was urged to tell what made her feel inferior some four years ago, she merely answered, "Oh, I don't know. I just did." In conference with the father concerning Betty's previous school work several questions were put to him: "Who gave Betty the idea that she couldn't do things as well as other children did them? Did she have some outstanding disagreeable experience which had robbed her of her confidence? Was there any teacher in the lower grades who had been unkind or unfair to Betty?" At first quite meekly and quite unlike his usual bombastic self Mr. Roberts answered, "Perhaps I did. You know I love my children and want to give them every advantage. I'm a self-made man. I am strong-willed. *I* demand. Things in the home must go *my* way; *I* am master in my house." It was startling to note how in the few words he spoke he worked himself up from a quiet gentleman into a hard, domineering tyrant. The worker answered, "Well, you have made a mess of things. Whether this girl can be helped or not will depend a great deal upon you!"

Primary Causation.—This is a case of cramped personality caused by the exhibitionism of the father who had become inflated to the bursting point by his own ego.

Secondary Causation.—The young girl was possessed by a feeling that effort is futile.

Contributory Causation.—She had no guidance from her mother.

Support of Diagnosis

Betty had been born into a family of little prominence and of little means. There had been periods of poverty when the father had not known just where to turn. The sudden acquisition of money, position and publicity had caused in Mr. Roberts a real upheaval. Suddenly he had become a "somebody," indeed, not an ordinary "somebody" but a powerful "somebody." From the time he had been inspired by the settlement worker to the present that had been his goal. Had he not said at twelve, "I want to be somebody"? At the same time deep in his consciousness Mr. Roberts knew that he held his present prominent position more through political pull and favor than because of unusual merit and superior preparation. His world was not as secure to himself as it seemed to the outside. The seeds of insecurity were well planted in his mind. To offset the feeling of instability and to establish a feeling of security for himself he dominated everybody and every situation, under his control. This overpowering egoism of the father had caused Betty to hide within herself. As she grew older she wanted to escape from it all. To her childish mind

going away to school spelled escape. It is evident that
the mother felt the same pressure. The latter escaped in
thought through a new religion and in reality by leaving
the city when things became unbearable. It is probably
not a mere coincidence that Mrs. Roberts sought a new
religion at the same time that Betty expressed the philosophy, "Why should one work so hard? Where does it
get you? Push, push, push!" As a result of this philosophy Betty, no doubt, felt an aversion to work. Effort
was futile. The next step soon followed. She felt inadequate.

If the mother in the situation had been stronger and
had been capable of standing her ground she could and
probably would have assisted Betty in facing issues.
Instead, Mrs. Roberts herself showed definite weakness.
Not only did she run away from real facts but she also
encouraged Betty not to meet situations as they came.

In the mother's case there were compensatory gestures
in many directions. Compensation took the form of outward conduct. She gained a feeling of equality by assuming the outward attributes of the certain level of
society which she wished to emulate. Beautiful clothes,
a house furnished according to a certain scale of wealth,
a fashionable school in the East for her daughter all
helped her to secure a feeling of equality of position. All
these compensations were a pose to convince herself and
the world at large that she really belonged to a certain
group.

Betty had no such outlets and being an adolescent she
could not find an answer to it all. Therefore, she became
pessimistic, unsocial and antagonistic. The school Betty
was attending was the choice of her father. Betty reacted

to the school and her fellow students as she would have liked to react to her father. In other words she gave vent to her feelings in the school. She hated the school and everything and every one connected with it. Only by doing poorly in her classes could she be released from school and home and gain her opportunity for being her real self, relieved from the domination of her egotistical father.

TREATMENT

Remedial measures in this case were of an unusually delicate nature. Three personalities had to be reckoned with, Mr. Roberts, Betty and Mrs. Roberts. It was necessary that Mr. Roberts recognize and admit his egotistic domination of his household and that he be made aware of the pernicious effect it was having upon his daughter's development. This remedy alone was a tremendous task because Mr. Roberts had been playing the rôle of one giving orders, not of one taking them. Betty, on the other hand, had to be made to see the fallacy of trying to escape from the situation she was in. Sooner or later in the normal process of growing up she would have to learn to face the disagreeable. This was an excellent time to learn. Because she had acquired a feeling of inferiority and inadequacy and had lost the joy of a piece of work well done, confidence had to be restored. Mrs. Roberts, too, had to be won over to a change of attitude toward Betty's problems.

The keynote of the remedial treatment was *encouragement*.

The case-worker was the only person who had the temerity to paint the picture in its true colors to Mr.

Roberts. It was not long before it became apparent that he had his vulnerable spot. He disclosed that the veneer of his greatness had been pierced, and, as is characteristic of his type, he became humble and voluble with explanations and good promises. While he was in a receptive mood it was made clear that his own bombastic egoism was the cause of Betty's difficulties and that overbearing conceit had crushed Betty to the point of abject discouragement and failure. Only by the greatest kindness, consideration and encouragement could the former attitude give way to one of confidence and ability to do. Mr. Roberts was not to urge his daughter to do well because her father was a great man and her failure would bring disgrace upon him, but he must humble himself and seek for the good points in Betty and praise her accordingly. He was advised that penalty cards for work poorly done would not be sent to the home. They would be kept in the office and showed to Betty only when it seemed that they would help rather than discourage her.

The mother was urged to refrain from interference with the plan. Through her, Betty must be directed to pick out the best things in the school and to get in touch with some of the many activities offered, instead of picturing the advantages of an eastern finishing school.

It was obvious that the craving on the part of Betty to get away from everything in her immediate surroundings must be satisfied. She, in her ignorance, was asking to be expelled so that she might go to boarding school. When arguments were presented she was clever enough to see that expulsion from a reputable high school would close the doors of the very schools into which she eagerly sought entrance. It was not difficult, furthermore, to persuade her that it would be a bit of folly to have her very first experience away from home extend over a period of nine months.

As many of the girls of her class were planning to attend Scout camp during the following summer, it was suggested that Betty try camp life for a month or more with the hope that the tension in the home would be relieved and there would be normal contact with girls of her own age. This plan was welcomed.

All Betty's instructors were consulted and their cooperation was sought in substituting encouragement in every possible way for failure. In order that Betty might gain a feeling of success commendation was given for any effort, however small, and praise was expressed for any task which was well done.

Betty was surrounded by encouragement and it was not long before her classmates did not appear as distasteful to her and the school was not the object of hatred it had been formerly. Progress was slow and there were many regressions in school work on Betty's part and in spirit and attitude on the father's part. There were times when every one had to start all over again. But it was encouraging to note progress in attention to work, completion of exercises and passing of tests.

At the end of the year three credits had been gained and one lost but Betty had done more than make credits: she had established friendly relations with her group and the instructors.

She started her vacation with a glimmer of enthusiasm and expressed a real desire to participate in the experiences of camp. The result of the summer away from home and of the life out in the open accomplished a great deal in improving her appearance and restoring her confidence. Minor awards were material evidence to her that she was capable of doing something well.

What a different girl she was in appearance at the beginning of her sophomore year! There was no shifting of eye, nor drooping of head. Betty entered the office, with a smile of greeting and a keen look in her eye. She started the year in her classes with enthusiasm and she entered into some extracurricular activities.

The Music Club caught her interest and she worked well on the program committee.

Mr. Roberts, of course, was egocentric and domineering but he had begun to take pride in Betty's achievement and because she was doing reasonably well she, *his* child, was shown off to his friends. His actions and attitude of course reflected his own egoism but this type of conduct was more comfortable and more encouraging to Betty than formerly.

The next years of school were completed with average grades. After graduation Betty started specialization in music. Reports came back to the school that she is now one of the most popular girls in the conservatory not only with the girls but also with young men. Adjustment seems to be permanent after four years.

CHAPTER XI

SUSAN was a freshman carrying a regular course of her own choosing—English, science, mathematics, French and elementary design. At the end of the first semester she passed English and French and received "incomplete" in the three other subjects. The second semester was started with Susan out of step with the majority of her class and instead of completing the work of the previous semester she proceeded to fail in those subjects which she had passed.

INVESTIGATION OF SCHOOL LIFE

Her instructors made the following reports:

English.—If Susan could keep her mind on the work at hand she would be an interesting and good pupil. It is difficult to help her for she refuses to coöperate and will not follow directions. If she is given suggestions or criticism she gets sulky and stops working.

Elementary Design.—Susan has talent but her efforts are spasmodic. Her attitude toward the work is exceedingly superficial. She is supersensitive. I find her very delightful as long as everything is going exactly as she would like it to go. She responds quickly to praise but she expects praise whether she deserves it or not.

216

French.—Susan has ability and she tells me that she is eager to learn French so that she may converse with her father and may plan to study art abroad. She is not passing in her work and she fails every test I give. Susan often says, "Please tell me what's wrong. I want to improve; I don't know what's the matter with me." When I reveal to her the fact that she is not putting forth any effort but is dreaming her time away, she seems very much surprised and says, "I thought I was working." Susan appears to long for complete lack of restraint.

Science.—Susan has ability but she is failing miserably. Sulkiness, moody spells and an antagonistic battling against life mark her behavior in my class.

Mathematics.—Susan feels that she cannot do the work in this class. She also says that she is inferior to the other members of the class and there is no use trying. This attitude inhibits her. Most of the time is spent in daydreaming.

Tests

Mental Tests.—In the Otis Higher Examination Susan's score made her I.Q. 115 (class median, 111.2).

ANALYSIS OF TERMAN GROUP TESTS OF MENTAL ABILITY

Test	Number Correct	Number Attempted	Perfect Score
Information	11	15	20
Best Answer	22	22	22
Word Meaning	21	26	30
Logical Set	11	15	20
Arithmetic	2	7	12
Sentence Meaning	10	11	24
Analogies	13	14	20
Mixed Sentences	9	10	18
Classification	11	15	18
Number Series	6	9	12

Chronological age: 15 years 1 month
Mental age: 13 years 2 months

In the Inglis Vocabulary Test her score was 67 (class median, 66).

Susan made a comprehension score of 40 on the Monroe Silent Reading Test (class median, 35).

Arithmetic Tests.—Susan's scores in the Reavis-Breslich tests are given in the table:

DETAILED RESULTS OF REAVIS-BRESLICH DIAGNOSTIC TESTS IN THE FUNDAMENTAL OPERATIONS OF ARITHMETIC AND IN PROBLEM SOLVING

Test	Number Correct	Number Attempted	Susan's Score
Tests I—VIII			
Addition	3	4	3
Subtraction	4	5	2
Multiplication	1	2	1
Division	2	2	2
Addition and Subtraction of Fractions	1	5	1
Multiplication and Division of Fractions	1	3	1
Placing Decimal Point in Multiplication	0	0	0
Placing Decimal Point in Division	0	0	0
Score I—VIII	13	21	10
Test IX: Problems without Numbers.	1	2	1
Test X: Problems with Numbers	3	3	3
TOTAL			14

Median for VA (I—X) — 15.6

Present Physical Condition

Susan was found to weigh twelve pounds less than normal for her age and height. Her pulse on standing was 68; after exercise, 96. Her nutrition was reported poor as was also her nail hygiene. She was taking from two to three hours of exercise a day. Her sleep at night was restless and was said to be from 11:30 P.M. to 7:00 A.M.

SOCIAL RECORD IN SCHOOL

Susan participated in all athletic activities and was a real part of her group. If teams were to be selected she was among the first chosen because she excelled in all types of gymnastic work—esthetic dancing, swimming, hockey and apparatus work. In play Susan was vivacious, happy and satisfied. There seemed to be a complete change in countenance and bearing while she was participating in sports.

Mother's Story

Mrs. Johnson showed both distress and surprise at Susan's failing record. She said that Susan had always hated arithmetic so that she had anticipated that there might be difficulty with high-school mathematics but she could not understand her poor work in English. From early childhood straight through the elementary grades Susan had loved English and had always written delightful poems and charming stories which she illustrated. Quite irrelevantly Mrs. Johnson continued, "Susan has had an inferiority feeling since she was seven or eight years old and I could shake her for it. She can hold up her head with the best of them. Of what should she be ashamed? We come from a fine, cultured family and she has good blood in her." From the rest of her conversation it was apparent that the same type of resentment and sulkiness shown in school was being displayed at home for Susan did not want to help with the house work and would not coöperate in any home projects. She refused to be orderly and systematic about even her own room. Mrs. Johnson could not understand her an-

COMPOSITE PERSONALITY RATING OF SIX INSTRUCTORS

	High		Medium		Low	
Refined		x				Coarse
Modest			x			Vain
Democratic		x				Snobbish
Cheery					x	Peevish
Patient					x	Irritable
Courteous			x			Discourteous
Friendly		x				Reserved
Cordial			x			Indifferent
Sociable		x				Unsociable
Imaginative	x					Prosaic
Altruistic				x		Selfish
Coöperative					x	Combative
Open-to-suggestion					x	Opinionated
Optimistic					x	Pessimistic
Keenly alive				x		Apathetic
Loquacious			x			Taciturn
Self-poised						Flighty
Calm			x			Excitable
Trustful				x		Jealous
Well-spoken			x			Gossipy
Common-sense				x		Lacking in judgment
Frank		x				Underhanded
Honest	x					Dishonest
Reliable	x					Unreliable
Reasonable					x	Unreasonable
Prompt				x		Dilatory
Industrious				x		Idle
Attentive					x	Inattentive
Steady					x	Intermittent

tagonism and was eager for the assistance of the school.

Susan's Version of the Difficulty

Susan's explanation was just an incoherent story of "I don't know why I don't get along because I think that I am trying. None of my teachers like me because I'm not smart. I never could do arithmetic and I don't see why I have to take it in high school. I'll never need it because I'm going to be an artist."

She told reluctantly that her father and mother had been divorced for five years and that she loved her father and thought that he was wonderful. How she longed to live with him but the court had decreed that she must live with her mother from Sunday night until Friday night! Week-ends were days of joy and happiness for then she was with him. Susan hated her mother because she felt that she was a poser and a social climber. She was always gadding about and never stayed home to take care of her. She left Susan at home alone too much. Disharmony was apparent in every sentence uttered by Susan.

Interpretation

Susan is having difficulty with all school subjects. Her rating in tests of reading, vocabulary and general intelligence place her above the median of her class. There is sufficient background in these fields so that high-school work should be carried on successfully. In mathematics, however, there is definite disability. She has practically no knowledge of fractions and decimals and has little skill in the various operations that are involved in addition, subtraction and multiplication in the simplest form.

There is a marked personality disturbance. Sulkiness, antagonistic attitude toward teachers and her mother, excessive daydreaming and a feeling of shame and inferiority show a fundamental emotional upset.

Her physical condition is not up to par. She is underweight, has evidences of poor nutrition and she bites her nails which is indicative of nervousness. Her hours of rest are not sufficient. She does not get enough sleep to enable her to attack her work with vim.

The feeling of inferiority and inadequacy is apparently deep-seated, for the mother stated that it had been evident as early as the seventh year of her life. There is a definite conflict caused by the separation from her father and shown in the hatred for the mother.

INVESTIGATION OF LIFE OUTSIDE OF SCHOOL

The Johnson family numbered four, the mother, Susan and two older sisters. Both the older girls were attending college and were students of more than average attainment. Mrs. Johnson was a college graduate and an artist of considerable prominence. For this reason people of position and culture were entertained in the home and Susan had close, stimulating contacts with them.

The family occupied an old apartment located in a fairly good neighborhood. The home itself was handsomely furnished. The unusually good pictures, the fine though worn oriental rugs, a Steinway baby grand piano, a large library of well-selected books were all evidences of refinement and culture and bespoke the affluence of former days. Their whole plane of living was lower than formerly because Mrs. Johnson's alimony was small and although she earned some money through her art the combined income was not sufficient to provide many of the luxuries of life.

There seemed to be a wholesome spirit of comradeship between the mother and the older girls. Susan alone showed antagonism and resentment. She resented everything, the place in which they lived, the made-over dresses she wore, her mode of living and the fact that she was a member of the household.

Everything pointed to an orderly and systematized home. The food for Susan was wholesome and well cooked. Susan's hours of rest, however, were not sufficient. Seldom did she have more than seven and a half hours in bed even on school nights. Mrs. Johnson had ceased to demand that Susan go to bed on time because, as she said, "There was so much disagreement and such an upheaval that she had given up the fight months ago."

Susan was exceedingly active. In addition to sports at school she played tennis, roller-skated and walked a mile to and from school. Again in play there was evidence that she was happy.

EARLY HISTORY AND DEVELOPMENT

The family histories on both sides showed good, sturdy English stock. Good breeding and education went back many generations. Both paternal grandparents had been college graduates. On both sides of the family several cases of nervousness, manic depressive tendencies and unstability were reported.

Physical History

Birth and physical development were normal. The family record showed that Susan weighed six and a quarter pounds at birth, was breast fed, walked at thirteen months, had her first tooth at six months and talked at fourteen months. The diseases of childhood, measles, whooping cough and chickenpox came before she was nine years old. None of these diseases seemed to have left any noticeable permanent physical defects. At the age of ten, abscesses of the lower lid of the eye and of the ear and a period of frequent colds had caused some absence from school.

Emotional History

As a child Susan was a bit timid with older people but she had never had any difficulty in making friends and playing with children of her own age.

Until the time of the divorce Susan had appeared very even-tempered and quite amiable. There had been no display of tantrums or behavior difficulties of any sort. She had always been of a fine, sensitive disposition and every one said that Susan had shown artistic ability from the time she could first hold a pencil.

The divorce of her parents was a real shock to the child for she was devoted to her father. When he ceased to live with the family she grieved silently. Only once or twice did she ask, "Why doesn't father stay with us?" The mother tried to explain the whole affair and to tell Susan that the court had given her to the mother and that she did not belong to the father any more. Susan rebelled. She wanted to belong to him. It is essential

to note that Susan at this time never admitted to the
children in the neighborhood that her father did not
live with them. Excuses were made for his absence. He
was away on a long trip or he had to stay in the city
because his work was exceedingly confining. Her mother
overhearing her fabricating such yarns had asked her
why she had made up such stories when she knew they
were not true. Susan wept and explained that she was
ashamed to let them know that she didn't have a father
and a real home. All the other children with whom she
played came from real homes. Whenever Mrs. Johnson
talked over these matters Susan became angry, insolent
and disrespectful. It was not long before the mother
began to ignore entirely what she termed "Susan's
spells."

Five years passed by and on the surface Susan appeared to be reconciled to the family arrangement. During the summer between the elementary school and the
high school, without any forewarning, Susan read in the
paper of the marriage of her father to a woman of considerable means. She burst into tears, wept hysterically
and refused to be comforted. Time and time again she
reiterated, "It isn't fair, it isn't fair. If I had been with
him it wouldn't have happened." A month later by
court decree Susan's living arrangements were changed
again. It was stated that the child should live with her
mother for five days and the other two days of each
week with the father. Proximity of the suburb in which
Mr. Johnson lived made the trip for every week-end very
easy and convenient. So it came about that Susan lived
during the school week in a very modest way while she
spent the remaining two days of the week in a home of

luxury where everything was done for her. To Susan the best part of it all was that she was with the father whom she adored. Such an existence in itself is disturbing enough but to add to the disintegration, the second Mrs. Johnson never lost an opportunity in sowing seeds of dissension. She talked constantly of Susan's mother's incompetency in keeping a home together and in holding her husband. She hinted that Susan had been positively neglected during her early years and stated that she thought that at the present time Susan was very poorly dressed, considering the amount of money her father gave to her mother for dress allowance.

Unhappiness, resentment and shame kept Susan in turmoil.

School History

The first school experience was in a good public school, progressive in method. During her eighth year while she was still in the third grade a case of chickenpox caused a few weeks of absence. Susan says that she never liked arithmetic after that time. She never knew just what the other children were doing. She was confused and lost. About the same time the mother's divorce case was in the courts and for that reason her whole attention was occupied with affairs quite foreign to Susan's progress and adjustment in school.

The child's teachers reported that Susan seemed to lose interest in school, she showed a decided change in disposition and she would sit and dream much of the time. Although the work of the grade was not very well done, nevertheless, because she was bright and quick it was thought wisest not to have her repeat the grade. In this incident we see the beginning of arithmetical weakness.

A move from the small town to a big city added its burden to school progress. Susan did not want to leave and she had begged to live with her favorite aunt, who had been devoted to her from babyhood. She had confided to her aunt that she was afraid to go to the city because she was convinced that she could never do her arithmetic and would be so ashamed before the other children. Furthermore, what could she say when girls asked where her father was. All the other girls would have fathers. If her father were dead, it would be different but she was ashamed to let them know that he would not live with them. Sympathetically aware of Susan's lack of adjustment, her aunt had joined forces with her and had urged that the child be left with her for a year but to no avail. As a result, Susan started school in her new surroundings fearful, ashamed and unhappy. Quite naturally her efforts were only half-hearted and her accomplishment was only fair. At first disinterest was evident especially in arithmetic. Soon disinterest became colored with emotion and Susan became nervous and disagreeable whenever she had to do problems. It was only a short time before she said that she could not do what the other children did, she did not know as much as they did and she was ashamed to go to school. For the next few years adjustment in school had been very difficult. Through the understanding of competent teachers, however, there had been gradual improvement in attitudes of work and actual accomplishment. At the end of the eighth grade everything seemed to be working out rather well in Susan's development. Her recommendation to the high school mentioned weakness in arithmetic but strength in every other subject.

Primary Causation.—An emotional perversion in the form of shame was brought on by the divorce of her parents.

Secondary Causation.—Susan felt an active resentment toward her mother.

Tertiary Causation.—Much time was given to daydreaming in school with resulting failure.

Contributory Causation.—(*a*) Illness and absence during the third grade put her out of step in arithmetic. The weakness caused a feeling of inferiority every time mathematics was presented.

(*b*) Poor nutrition and too little sleep kept her underweight and did not give her the physical energy necessary to meet with any sort of zest a task which she disliked.

(*c*) The week-ends spent with the father and the stepmother kept the wound ever open.

Support of Diagnosis

Until the age of eight Susan had been a happy, contented little girl, sensitive and fine in make-up. Divorce came into the family. To one of Susan's impressionableness the divorce was a severe shock. Shame and distress filled her mind and soul because the adored father was removed from the home. In countless ways she showed that the new family arrangements went against the grain. Her little playmates must never know that the father did not live with them. So she fabricated plausible stories. When forced to go into new surroundings, consumed with fear and shame she asked, "How shall I explain to the girls that father does not live with us? The girls will come from *real* homes." On every hand there is evidence that the broken-home situation could not be faced. It is very natural that her genuine devotion to her father should make her believe that her mother had been at fault in the whole affair. As a result she felt resentment and dislike for her mother. Whatever the mother did was wrong. No explanations offered by the mother eased matters, kindnesses went unappreciated. These attitudes cannot be explained away by human meanness and perversity. They are the result of a permanent hurt to a sensitive, artistic nature and of the lack of understanding of it all. In school, as a consequence, Susan could not coöperate, did not feel equal to, appeared to be battling against the unconquerable forces of life. Her attention was not upon school work but upon finding an answer to the insoluble home problem. Her family life was different. No wonder she was termed "superficial in her reactions to school work"!

At the very time when she was suffering mentally and emotionally from shock, physical illness had caused absence from school to complicate matters. She was at a very crucial point in the learning process. In the third and fourth grades children begin to learn how to study. Arithmetic, especially, branches out into the more difficult types of learning. Work in fractions and decimals is started. When the first, easy explanations were made Susan was not there. She admitted that from that time on she had never known what they were doing. Every child seemed to know more than she did. Again came the feeling of shame. The mother, too busy with her marital affairs, gave no heed nor consideration to the adjustment of the groping child. In school the teacher either did not sense the situation or ignored it. Susan was so bright that she would pick up the knowledge in the next grade. So began the process of applying the veneer and utterly neglecting the fundamental disability. The move to another school made matters worse. New teachers had to have time to discover the weakness. But Susan's emotions were in no static state. She was afraid to have the weakness discovered. It was not long before Susan's fear had created a feeling of inferiority and actual resistance and rebellion came when arithmetic was presented. To escape disagreeable reality Susan resorted to daydreaming.

Susan's physical condition may account for some lack of drive. She had too little sleep for a growing girl and she was noticeably underweight. Whatever energy she possessed was spent in strenuous sports and games. There was, in fact, little physical drive left for school work. Her physical lassitude was great enough to keep her from overcoming her emotional conflicts and attacking uninteresting school work.

Furthermore, the adjustment each week to two entirely different modes of living was upsetting and very enervating. Very few adults are sufficiently well-balanced to accommodate themselves to such an existence. How could Susan be expected to keep her equilibrium, for all life was entirely out of perspective? Changes had to be made too rapidly. After the week-end filled with luxuries, service and attention, Susan's mind was centered upon many things far removed from science, mathematics and

French. (How deep were the imprints of the stepmother's taunts!) Over and over in her mind Susan mulled these accusations. She was convinced now that she had always been correct in her conjectures. Her mother was not like other mothers. She had neglected her, she had dressed her poorly, she had been inadequate in every home relationship. Rightly Susan had suffered shame and humiliation. The result was a whirlpool of emotions with Susan, sensitive and impressionable, at its very vortex.

TREATMENT

What can be done for a young child who is the victim of a broken home and who feels the disgrace of separation so keenly? To change the attitudes of the separated parents is impossible for if attitudes toward each other could have been changed there would probably have been no divorce. The whole affair was a delicate matter. (Remedial work had to start with some of the tangible things which could be corrected with great benefit to Susan. Effort was immediately directed toward overcoming underweight and loss of sleep. A strict diet including protein, iron and vitamins A, B, C, was made out by the home economics teacher. (Mrs. Johnson eagerly followed the program. Susan's bed time was changed from eleven-thirty to nine-thirty. Full coöperation was given by the whole family even though the change necessitated some rearrangements in the family sleeping quarters. Susan's bedroom was now the one farthest from the living room so that she would not be disturbed when the older sisters entertained their friends.

Mathematics could never be carried successfully until

definite remedial work in the fundamentals of arithmetic was started. The instructor reported that it was amazing how very little Susan actually knew about arithmetic. Fractions, decimals and the simplest kind of problem had to be taught. It was a slow, discouraging process at times, for Susan saw no use in the hard task. The personality of the mathematics teacher helped to win over the child and she began to put forth effort to please the teacher. It took months of hard, steady grind but, finally, there was a change of attitude and she liked not only the teacher but mathematics. At no time during this remedial teaching would Susan permit her friends to know that she was doing extra work. She had a feeling of shame that she had to do it. Often she asked the teacher after an especially good bit of work, "Do I look stupid now?"

In three things Susan could excel, in art, swimming and rhythms. General school interest was stimulated through the making of posters and through competition in a gymnastic exhibition. An appeal for good scholarship was made through the desire of Susan's father that she succeed scholastically. To please him she put forth effort in English and French especially.

It was comparatively easy to do these tangible things. The fact still remained that the fundamental difficulty was a feeling of shame and emotional upset about the separation of her parents. No permanent results would come unless shame were eradicated.

Much would have been gained if the week-end trips could have been discontinued, if the father could have been made conscious of the fact that these trips with the conversations which occurred were positively detrimental to the child and were contributing causes of her failure, and if the child could have lived with one parent or the other all the time. The father refused to have any communication with the school, except to pay the bills. Through Susan, he informed the school that the court had assigned the care and education of the child to the mother and had allotted two days of the week to him. He wanted the arrangements continued as decreed. This channel for help was definitely closed and one source of maladjustment was constantly fed.

(In simple language and as tactfully as possible Susan was urged to bring her whole trouble into the open and talk about it. The virtues of Mrs. Johnson were extolled. Surely the desperate fight her mother had made to keep her as a child did not give evidence of neglect nor could the mother be so utterly incompetent when she had kept a home together for her family for so many years. In order to get sufficient funds to keep up her home life Mrs. Johnson had been forced to leave Susan alone at times. Many proofs of real sacrifice on the mother's part were brought into evidence.

(Divorce was discussed very openly. It was shown to Susan that unfortunate as it may be divorce is very common and many children are victims of broken homes. In fact, several of her own classmates came from the same type of home. Nothing could change that fact now. She would have to accept everything just as it was and make the best of it. Going to live with her father and stepmother would not bring true happiness because Susan was too sensitive and fine not to have an innate loyalty to her mother. Such were the arguments used. (Susan was too young, perhaps, to understand the whole argument but she did respond to the encouragement and understanding which she felt that she was receiving. A combination of the above factors in some way increased her desire to put forth effort and at the close of the semester she had passed everything but French.

Of her own volition the following year she repeated French and took the next course in mathematics. This was proof of definite growth.

Her whole history through high school was a series of periods of fairly good work and times of terrific slump and discouragement. Socially she made a better adjustment and lost the feeling of shame in part and was able to discuss divorce with little emotion, outwardly, at least. With extra work in summer school she graduated with her class.

Can there ever be a permanent cure? It is doubtful. The damage done to a young, impressionable child by two so-called intelligent, cultured adults has left a permanent scar.

CHAPTER XII

INFERIORITY FEAR: THE CASE OF FLORENCE SCHILLING

FLORENCE SCHILLING, seventeen years of age and a member of the high school for three years, was carrying as subjects English III, mathematics II, ancient history and home economics. At a time near the end of the first semester she came into the office with the request that her report card be kept at school for a week at least as she knew that she would fail in one subject and did not want the failure to be sent home because the family would call her "Dummy" again and she could not endure it. At the time of the interview her hands were cold and clammy, her eyes were very wide open and suffused with tears, her face was flushed and her muscles were tense and rigid.

INVESTIGATION OF PRESENT SCHOOL LIFE

The reports of Florence's teachers follow:

History.—Florence is interested and faithful and she tries to coöperate in getting satisfactory results. Because of her emotional and moody make-up she finds it difficult at times to work effectively. She appears at times slow of comprehension and has a hard time recalling her material. Quiz results: (1) score of 28 out of possible 56; (2) score of 24 out of possible 36; (3) score of 26 out of possible 44. I have tried to have her read one paragraph then pause and go over the content to herself. Florence needs to relax from her high tension.

English III.—This pupil lacks confidence in herself but she puts forth a most sincere effort. She is prompt with her work but requires a much longer period of time than the average to complete a task. She is slow to express herself and shows confusion. She is never quite up to credit level.

Mathematics II.—Florence works slowly and nervously. She is easily discouraged and she is never quite sure of anything, usually wavering from one answer to another. Patient effort on her part and much teacher help have made it possible for her to complete the work with the rest of the class. It is difficult to understand Florence because she never does as well as her ability and effort would lead one to expect.

Home Economics.—Florence has ability but she works intermittently. This lack of concentration does not seem to be due to any lack of willingness to work and a sincere desire to understand but rather to a nervous tension which she exhibits at all times in class but to a greater degree during recitation or test periods. Although she seems to know her material when I talk to her she has failed every test this semester and is now below credit level.

Tests

Reading Tests.—The scores on three tests were:

Test	Florence's Score	Median, X*
Monroe Silent Reading Test Comprehension (Form 1)	23	26
Thorndike-McCall Reading Scale Comprehension	61	62.5
Inglis Vocabulary	70	63

* Tenth-grade medians are given because Florence is in the first semester of the eleventh grade.

Mental Tests.—The Terman Group Tests of Mental Ability showed Florence's I.Q. to be 91 (mental age of 14 years, 7 months); while the results of the Otis Self-Administering Test put it at 98 (median of her class, 115).

DETAILED RESULTS OF THE REAVIS-BRESLICH DIAGNOSTIC TESTS IN THE FUNDAMENTAL OPERATIONS OF ARITHMETIC AND IN PROBLEM SOLVING

Test	Florence's Score	Median, X A
Tests I—VIII	42	44.07
Test IX: Problems without Numbers	2	6.63
Test X: Problems with Numbers...	6	9.82
TOTAL	50	60.14
Median, Grade VIII	51.2	

RECORD CARD OF DOWNEY INDIVIDUAL WILL-TEMPERAMENT TEST
Devised by June E. Downey, Ph.D. (World Book Co., Publishers, Yonkers-on-Hudson, New York).

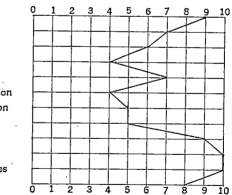

The examiner comments on the test: "Florence works at relatively high speed and is at the time capable of interested, careful and sustained effort. She is outwardly flighty and decidedly quick, yet there are other traits

which serve to control these impulsive tendencies and enable her to put forth careful, controlled effort."

Present Physical Condition

Florence had normal sight and hearing but weighed fifteen pounds less than the average for her height and age. Her pulse measured 96 when she was standing and after exercise, 140. She had a palpable thyroid gland and there was evidence of goiter. There was some tendency toward indigestion, thought by the physician to be a result of nervousness.

Social Record in School

Social activities in school were confined to the drama club where she was a spectator rather than a participant. During her daily walks to and from school she had normal friendly relations with the girls from her neighborhood. As yet her voluntary friendships were almost entirely confined to girls of fourteen or fifteen years who were in her classes at school. Activities in sports were average.

A composite rating of personality traits made by faculty members and Mrs. Schilling very definitely showed Florence as: cheerful, patient, friendly, social, courteous, modest, open to suggestion, frank, apathetic, inclined to follow, democratic, exceedingly nervous and excitable, emotional, intermittent in effort, honest, reliable and reasonable.

Mrs. Schilling's Version of the Difficulty

Both parents felt keen disappointment in Florence. Every advantage and every care had been given to their oldest child but in view of her school failures they had come to the conclusion that they were forced to admit that she was stupid and not as bright as the other children. Once they had expected great things of her but from now on they would just look for nothing. Mrs. Schilling gave way to her emotions and wept bitterly whenever she discussed her daughter.

Florence's Version of the Difficulty

Florence said that she tried as hard as it was possible for her to do but she just didn't seem to be able to get the work as others did. There was so much to do that she was "hurried and flurried" all the time. She must be the "dummy" they thought her to be at home. But she felt that it was no sign of stupidity that she was older than the other girls in her grade. She couldn't help that she had been ill and had lost time. When she had failed French and mathematics she had not felt so hopeless because a great many people had difficulty with those subjects. But to fail home economics was too much! She had always planned to be an interior decorator and the work in home economics was the very thing she loved to do. What was she to do? Was she to admit that she couldn't finish high school?

Interpretation

Evidence to date shows a learning difficulty in all classes. Emphasis is laid on Florence's lack of confidence, her nervous tension, slowness and discouragement by all teachers.

With the exception of the Inglis vocabulary test all scores are lower than the norm for X A grade. The intelligence quotient according to the Otis test is seventeen points below the median for her class. Yet none of the scores are so low that one should anticipate complete scholastic breakdown.

The results of the Downey Will-Temperament Test are at variance with the teachers' reports. The test shows "freedom from load" as above average yet teachers mention tension, lack of confidence and discouragement. Elements of weakness shown by test are high score in "Motor Inhibition," below average score in "Speed of Decision," "Finality of Judgment," "Reaction to Contradiction" and "Resistance to Opposition." The above results may account for wavering and indecision in class work. Points of strength are "Speed of Movement," "Coordination of Impulses" and "Volitional Perseveration." These latter results are diametrically opposed to teacher-comments.

There is evidence of a marked physical weakness of an endocrine nature with resulting underweight, rapid heart and nervous indigestion.

A feeling on the part of both parents and Florence that the latter is stupid had caused serious emotional distress in both mother and daughter.

Social relationships seem normal. The fact, however, that Florence associates with girls younger than herself may be due to grouping in the classes or to neighborhood conditions or to immaturity.

INVESTIGATION OF LIFE OUTSIDE OF SCHOOL

Florence's whole manner of living was wholesome and simple. Her meals were regular and well balanced and from the report of the mother she was in bed for more than nine hours a night. Amusement and entertainment were confined to week-ends and were of a very simple nature: small parties with girls, an occasional theater and normal church duties. Exercise was taken systematically, gymnasium work at school, a good walk to and from school, and games of tennis and golf. Although she would not have been classified as an excellent athlete, she did some sports rather well and thoroughly enjoyed playing games.

The Schilling home was modern, well kept and had the marks of culture of the home of the average professional gentleman. Good magazines and books were plentiful and gave every evidence of being used. The whole atmosphere of the home was comfortable and inviting.

There were three children younger than Florence, one girl and two boys. The younger children seemed more stolid and better poised than their older sister. Both Mr. and Mrs. Schilling were well educated and it seemed as if they had taken a serious and sensible view of training their children. The father was about nineteen years older than the mother and was a professional man of some ability who had been financially successful. Mrs. Schilling was an exceedingly nervous person, inclined to weep easily. A member of Mrs. Schilling's family reported that during Florence's early childhood, Mrs. Schilling's nervousness had grown alarmingly worse as she had experienced several severe nervous shocks. The mother and her children had been alone in the house when burglars entered and forced her at the point of a revolver to open a wall safe. At another time, one of the younger children at the age of two had run along a pier and jumped off the end into twenty feet of water. The child had been rescued but resuscitation had been difficult and there had been a long period of agony for the frantic mother.

EARLY HISTORY AND DEVELOPMENT

Physical History

Until the age of six years Florence's health had been exceedingly good and she had been normal in every respect. During her seventh year she had chickenpox and a mild case of influenza followed by serious bronchitis. During the winter of her eighth year several severe attacks of tonsilitis left her with muscular rheumatism. At eleven years of age she suffered from a hard case of diphtheria followed closely by measles. For a year following this siege Florence was weak and had a distinct cardiac murmur. Growth for a time was somewhat retarded and sexual maturity did not appear until her fifteenth year.

Emotional History

In babyhood, according to the father and mother, Florence had been a calm, quiet baby with no evidence of irritability, shyness or fears. Unfortunately, she had been a witness of the burglary in the home and also of the accident which had happened on the pier. These incidents, no doubt, made a deep and lasting impression on the child. The father reported that Florence began to show signs of nervousness similar to those displayed by Mrs. Schilling. Furthermore, two or three years of illness had proved to be a handicap which put the child not only physically but intellectually out of step with her playmates and at the same time caused an emotional and mental distress. She began to be worried as to whether she could keep up with others in her grade, for during the course of the elementary school she had lost two grades and she was older than the girls in her class. This emotionalism had carried over to her third year in high school.

In conference with Florence an endeavor was being made to find some reason for the nervous tension referred to by all teachers, but especially by the home economics teacher. When the questions were put to her: "What upsets you so much in home economics class? You enjoy the course and apparently you think you know your material. What makes you feel that you cannot pass your quizzes?" a most illuminating explanation was given.

Her remark was, "If I ever fail a test I can never pass *that* test, never, never." To the question, "Why?" quickly came the response, "Because the first failure is always before me." On further investigation the following facts were revealed: In any written work, if Florence read, for example, five questions which she could answer easily and then came upon a sixth question which she could not answer, such mental panic ensued that when she read over those questions which she had been able to answer correctly a few minutes before she could not think of the answers for any of the questions.

Later there was awareness of the same difficulty in physical work. During her freshman year in gymnasium she enjoyed track work and she did unusually well in the high jump. Once, however, on landing she twisted her ankle so that she suffered severe pain. Over a year later she tried the high jump with the bar inches below her former achievement and she not only had not been able to go over but could not even make the attempt. Her explanation to the instructor was that she could not pull up her knees because she felt a terrific pain in her ankle. Until that moment, however, she confessed that she had felt no pain in her ankle since her recovery from the fall over a year before.

Fear of such a paralyzing nature must have had its incipiency long before this time. When asked if she could remember the beginning of her overwhelming fear, Florence related a tale which might seem amusing and ludicrous if it were not for the seriousness of its implications and consequences.

While Florence was still in the sixth grade she was associating with several older girls who were attending high school and who were at the time studying physiology. These girls discovering that Florence was impressionable and excitable tried to impress their superiority upon her by describing details of their course in physiology. They gave in vivid detail the workings of the uvula. Dramatically they related cases in which the little tongue swelled up at night when the person was asleep and caused death by choking. The most disastrous results were reported to have occurred while individuals of certain types were chewing meat. The girls declared that Florence was definitely the type just mentioned.

The reaction to these stories was so great that for weeks Florence could not sleep at night. She grew thin and weak but her consuming fear was never revealed to any one. She tried to turn vegetarian but in vain. Forced by her parents to eat meat she had been in the habit of chewing it and then surreptitiously concealing it on a ledge under the table. Every day she secretly cleaned off the ledge. Her emotional upset was terrific during this period for she feared detection as well as disaster. By accident one day the maid discovered Florence cleaning off the ledge and reported the matter to Mrs. Schilling. The unusual action, of course, called forth an explanation from Florence. At that time the parents had had a chance to cope with the fear but they had given very little thought to the incident and had believed that they had cleared up the whole matter when they had remonstrated with Florence and had told her how silly, foolish and gullible she was. In fact, they had made a great joke of it and had repeated the incident to their friends in the presence of Florence. At the time Florence suffered from both the fear of disaster because of the uvula and the sting of caustic ridicule.

Scholastic History

All elementary school work had been taken in a conventional public school located in a beautiful residential section of a large city. School was a happy experience until the second grade when Florence had a series of diseases with ensuing absence. She passed into the third grade, however, but she began to lose confidence because she had missed so many things that the other children had had. During this grade an attack of muscular rheumatism caused her to be absent a great deal. For this reason it was thought best that she repeat the third grade. Again at eleven years old when she was in the fifth grade a case of diphtheria followed by measles caused her to miss a great deal of school so that there was need for her to repeat the fifth grade. So it was that Florence entered the high school at the age of fifteen. Her recommendations were only fair but no specific weaknesses were stated. Her first year in high school had proved almost fatal. At the end of one month it was necessary for her to drop French, one of her four subjects. During the first semester she successfully completed English I, mathematics I, and design. Her second semester was even more discouraging, a failure in mathematics and a condition in design. During the summer she carried French at summer school and received a passing grade of 80. Her second year started with French II, English II, repetition of mathematics I and general science (a freshman course). Within a few weeks it was advisable for her to drop French and devote her energy to three subjects for the rest of the school year. At the beginning of her third year Florence was permitted to take a full program: English III, mathematics II, modern history, and home economics. She was eager for the chance to try, saying that she felt confident that she could carry the work this year easily. It was failure in the home economics which prompted the whole investigation.

DIAGNOSIS

Primary Causation.—This is a case of a fear complex causing exaggerated inhibitions in both mental and physical work.

Contributory Causation.—A nutritional disorder exists in relation to endocrine trouble.

Support of Diagnosis

The evidence of a distinctly unbalanced emotional structure can be traced back very definitely to childhood.

The occasion of the development of this fear was probably a combination of exposure to a nervous mother, nervous shock received from witnessing two tragic episodes in the mother's life and two long periods of illness with loss of school work and subsequent loss of grade position. All these incidents had left their imprint of fear, a consuming, overwhelming fear which never left her free to do work of either a physical or mental nature because of strain and terrific inhibitions. In the period from seven to twelve or thirteen years there had been a constant striving on her part to maintain even physical equality. Because of this physical inequality, and being constantly out of step with her friends in school she worried and fretted that she could not keep up and therefore was going to lose more school and increase the distance between herself and girls of her own age. It probably was the fact that she felt the superiority of certain girls who had gone into high school that made her give credence to their nonsensical tales and caused her to suffer emotional torture because of them. Her self-confidence had been undermined. There was a constant worry that she might not measure up. Through ignorance the family added an extra burden by their lack of understanding. At the time when Florence was stirred emotionally over the little tongue, they had handled the matter poorly. Instead of clearing up the difficulty and relieving the fear and humiliation they had called her "silly" and had ridiculed her. She had become the target for their banter. The sting of that ridicule had gone deep into her consciousness and had made her have less confidence in her own judgment. In addition, the parents had become convinced that Florence was mentally inferior. They said, "Once they had expected great things from Florence but now they looked for nothing because they had been forced to admit that she was stupid." Nor had they kept this to themselves. Florence was fully aware of their attitude and feeling. Did she not say, "I must be the dummy they think I am at home?" "Don't send home my report card or they will call me dummy again!" She put up a nice defense for herself when she said, "It is no sign of stupidity that I am older than the other girls in my class; I was ill and lost time."

In school, when she was presented with a test either in scholastic or physical work her fear created a mild hysteria. If she came across something which she could not do or thought at first sight that she could not do, paralyzing fear blocked the normal flow of her thought and the task which had been simple the minute before became impossible. Having failed once she could not succeed in that same test. The fear of failure was ever present. The same hysteria was evident when she tried to high jump. Her muscles were paralyzed, she could not get her feet up because she felt the pain experienced over a year before. She was gripped by fear.

It is rather difficult to determine whether Florence's physical condition was the result of her fear or whether it was a contributory cause for her failure. She had a goiter with rapid heart, underweight and indigestion. The condition might well be an outgrowth of her nervous fear. Physicians state that "the primary cause of goiter is a weakened nervous system, and the struma is a secondary symptom." [1] Whether the goiter was the cause

---

[1] Israel Bram, *Goiter: Non-Surgical Types and Treatment* (New York, The Macmillan Company, 1924), p. 114.

or result in Florence's case, it was a definite deterrent. Added fear increased the goiter and it in turn reacted on the nervous system. So a vicious circle was established. Mental confusion and distress were resultant.

TREATMENT

Three things were necessary in an intelligent program of treatment: (1) It was absolutely imperative that a feeling of confidence, self-reliance and assurance be established; (2) contact with a medical specialist was needed; and (3) a light school program with plenty of relief periods had to be arranged.

It is one thing to tell a young girl that she must not get nervously upset and it is a much more difficult task to teach her poise and control. In conference with Florence her physical condition was made the basis for a recommendation that she drop home economics and use that period for rest and taking of extra nourishment. It was constantly kept before her that this recommendation was in no way connected with inability to carry a fourth subject or with any mental inadequacy whatsoever.

It was arranged with instructors that in all written work Florence be required to see but one question at a time and that special attention and encouragement be given to her until she had passed the first nervous reaction to any test.

In gymnasium work infinite patience was shown by the instructor in seeing that Florence overcame every physical obstacle. If she could not do a physical feat at once it was made a matter of little importance but the suggestion was made in the spirit of fun and play that she try it again.

Simple educational principles were discussed with her. It was made clear that the school was much more interested in her own personal development and growth than in a comparison of her work with that of other pupils; that it was not a question of whether she knew more or less than her neighbor but rather how much she herself had gained. This procedure had a most salutary effect.

There was need of a definite piece of work with the parents concerning the significance and importance of the "dummy" episode in Florence's development. They came to the realization that their lack of confidence in Florence was an absolute deterrent in restoring her faith in herself. Coöperation was solicited in keeping the thought constantly before Florence that she was just as bright and quick as other people and, further, that the idea of failure must never be even remotely suggested as a possibility.

A medical specialist gave her a thorough physical examination including a metabolism test and made the following report: "Metabolic rate: $+14$. The whole organism is working at too high a rate. Slight goiter. Rapid heart and loss of weight result of the thyroid condition. Much rest and wholesome dietary recommended. Treatment to be given at intervals."

Within a period of six weeks through the combined efforts of physician, home and school, definite evidence of relaxation was present. (1) At rest periods she slept soundly. (2) Instructors reported that she was less excitable, better poised, able to concentrate for longer periods and doing a much more competent piece of work. (3) The physician reported definite improvement in physical condition. (4) Mrs. Schilling had noticed an entire change in spirit and attitude around the home. Florence was happier. (5) The best evidence of improvement came in Florence's own statement: "Oh! I feel so much better and happier because I am not afraid and I am not worrying"—a short sentence but one fraught with the greatest meaning.

As the end of the school year drew near, Mrs. Schilling was questioned as to plans for the summer. On suggestion of the school Florence was placed in a small camp under the guidance of an intelligent director who understood the fundamental difficulties of her problem. This recommendation was made in order that Florence might be relieved from the nervous association at home, that she might enter into natural physical activities with normal girls and might see their normal reactions and that she might get away from the confusion, stress and strain of city life.

(Because fear, nervousness and lack of confidence were the basic causes of Florence's scholastic difficulty, it was believed that the scores in the standardized tests had probably been affected.) It was evident that Florence should be retested but there was hesitancy in proceeding with another testing program lest it be a distressing experience for her and hinder the progress which was being made. It was decided that a scheme must be worked out through which Florence herself would suggest retesting. Quite casually during a conference concerning matters wholly unrelated to school matters the conversation was cautiously directed to tests, adroitly the way was opened for Florence to mention her own tests. With a bit of hesitancy she asked, "Are those tests which I took once ever given again? I'd like to take them. I know that I could do much better now." The victory was won. The date was set with the utmost care and every precaution was taken to have conditions as perfect as possible. The tests were given in a quiet, private office and a feeling of easy companionableness was established before the tests were started.

Florence's whole manner of attack was one of natural interest. She was calm, alert and free. The results of the tests:

Test	Previous Score	Later Score	University High School Median for X A
Otis Self-Administering Test	I.Q. 98	I.Q. 116 [2]	I.Q. 116.7
Monroe Silent Reading Test (Comprehension)	23	33	29.4
Thorndike-McCall Reading Scale	61	65	62.5
Inglis Vocabulary	70	77	78

[2] Inconstancy of I.Q. is not an uncommon occurrence. It has been found that twenty and even thirty-five points' change in I.Q. is quite common! The data of this study seem to indicate that environment is quite dominant in determining the intelligence of a majority of children.—John Munroe, *The Inconstancy of the Intelligence Quotient and the Influence of Environment upon Intelligence*, dissertation (Department of Education, University of Chicago, August, 1928), pp. 239-240.

Florence came into the office three times to find out if her tests were scored. When she was told that her results were about normal she quickly asked, "Then I'm not really stupid?" She realized that the tests were merely a tangible proof of the statements of her instructors that she was improving.

At the end of the school year three subjects had been

passed creditably. She had received two cards of commendation during the period:

English.—Florence deserves commendation for the originality and initiative she displayed in her last English report.

History.—In a special report before the class Florence showed much care in organization and a greater degree of accuracy in her expression. The whole performance was most creditable.

After an interesting and invigorating summer in the woods Florence began school in the fall with four regular subjects—English, general biology, modern history and history of art. She had no difficulty in passing all subjects and she received an honor grade in history.

Her former record made it impossible for her to graduate in four years but she was perfectly satisfied to stay a fifth year, and at no time did the delay in graduation seem to have created any embarrassment or resentment.

After one year of college she was married, and from reports received at intervals she is living a normal adult life.

CHAPTER XIII

FOR any one to attempt to make sweeping generalizations or to derive principles of conduct which might be applied to all adolescent girls is presumptuous and futile. Yet in the course of years of work with girls certain types of problems are found to recur time and again.

This chapter will deal very briefly with some of the most outstanding, fundamental difficulties which appear.

It is with hesitation and with fear of misinterpretation that the very overworked and often misunderstood term "inferiority complex" is stated as the most frequent and most baffling problem with which one must cope.

According to the mental hygienist a complex has at its root an emotional conflict. The experiences which brought about the conflict may or may not have been recognized at the time they occurred but at any rate these experiences were pushed out of the way into the subconscious. At that time, the organism, although a struggle was made, could not make an adaptation and there came as a result an intense emotional conflict. All inferiority complexes are an admission of failure on the part of the individual to make a true and complete adaptation. All human beings, both old and young alike, are constantly endeavoring to adapt themselves to themselves, as it were. They are grasping constantly for evidence within themselves of being what they want to be and are not. This struggle in an acute form is present in maturing young girls especially. Many of them cannot endure to accept themselves as they find themselves. They desire to be different and the process of gaining self-satisfaction is most difficult. This enervating stress and strain seeks to relieve itself through compensatory conduct. Manifestations are legion.

Probably the most innocuous form of compensatory action is found among those adolescents who disguise their feelings of cowardice and self-depreciation by over-aggressiveness, self-aggrandizement, argumentation and contrariness. The conduct of the girl who must constantly dramatize herself, must be the center of attention and must taste the sweetness of dangerous adventure and "dare-devil" pranks is usually spurious. She is merely using these devices to cover up her fundamental admission of inferiority. Afraid to let the world know of her fear of incompetency, she cloaks herself with the veneer of superiority.

Such a case was Ruth. To the casual observer she was an unbearable snob, far too "high-brow" to indulge in the idle chitter-chatter of the group. The fact that she seldom entered into any social activity and that scholastically she ranked very low to all outward appearances was most inconsequential. Her superior bearing and evident tolerance of pupil and teacher alike made conversation with her a formal and stilted matter. Ruth's most consuming interest was genealogies. Her own family pedigree was her hobby. So important had become this subject that her vacation periods were spent almost entirely in digging out further evidence of her superior lineage. When Ruth did occasionally condescend to speak with her classmates the conversation seldom failed to include references to some famous personage to whom she was distantly related. Very few ever realized that beneath that unfriendly, impenetrable surface was a gnawing feeling of shame because of the inferior social position of her family, a longing for a close, intimate friend and a genuine desire for a higher scholastic standing. Thus it is that human beings present to the world only the compensating exterior for an inner struggle.

Another incident amusing yet pathetic will suffice to illustrate this point. Mrs. G———, distinctly *nouveau riche,* was making application for her daughter at a private school where admission was on a selective basis. Exquisiteness described her outward appearance. Her dress, manners, and speech paid tribute to an efficient social tutor. The tragedy of the refusal of admission, however, pierced the veneer, and vociferously she screamed, "My God, why isn't she to be accepted? She is a lady and everybody's equal. She has a fur coat and good clothes. I even got a chauffeur last week." Mrs. G——— is not unique. She represents a large class of individuals who compensate for lack of inner poise and self-assurance by material acquisitions.

Again most of the serious disciplinary cases in school are the outcome of dangerous overcompensation. Solution for a baffling, personal problem is craved. It consumes the whole being and becomes intolerable. Any and every type of escapade is resorted to in an endeavor to gain relief. School experiences show that truancy, stealing, adventurous wanderings and moral delinquencies are often the sequelæ of inferiority fear. The most brazen is often the most fearful.

All too common in our schools are the compensators who overwhelmed by a feeling of inadequacy make a tremendous effort to square themselves with themselves and live in a state of chronic anxiety, fear and worry. All too frequently if the compensation is not successful, there develops a pathological psychosis and at times in severe cases a chronic physical upset resulting in pathological neurosis.

Such a case was Florence Schilling (Chapter XII). Early in her school years she feared being out of step with her companions and began to worry whether she could ever keep up with the other children. She failed because she feared failure. The gripping, paralyzing fear created such inhibitions that she could not release any knowledge on topics which she understood thoroughly. Caught in the vortex of a vicious circle of worry and fear she was dangerously near the breaking point.

Sadie, too, was the victim of worry. With face drawn and wrinkled, she scuttled down the corridors, stooped over as if Atlas had suddenly shifted the world to her shoulders. Superior in scholastic work but unhappy and uncomfortable she mulled over in her mind her unsatisfactory social adjustment, for she could not mix comfortably with her fellows. The idle give and take of young people was a closed book to her. She confessed that she longed to have a "line" like the most sophisticated girls. She felt so inferior that she admitted that there was no reason at all why she should interest anybody, why any one should want to talk to her or to invite her to parties. Worried, unhappy, envious and almost desperate she became the object of self-torture and accusations. More and more she withdrew into herself. Hence, more and more difficult became the very contacts for which she longed. Satisfaction did not come through reality so relief was secured through the day dream. Studies were not quite as interesting and absorbing as they had been. The same picture recurring again and again broke the continuity of thought. In the dream world Sadie was gay, lovable and loving. Friends, both boys and girls, crowded around her and were entertained by her scintillating remarks. But the problem was not solved by her retreat into the dream. This refusal of facing reality merely aggravated the whole situation and made adjustment more difficult to attain. Cure could be effected only by forcing her to tackle the task of seeing things as they were and by guiding her to compensate through satisfactory achievements in sports and drama where intimate association with her fellows was compulsory.

It is not at all uncommon to find serious compensatory conduct among girls who belong to outstanding families in a community. Take for example, a girl whose father has not only a local but a national reputation in a specific field. While she is still in the pre-adolescent period, she often lives in the glow of reflected glory and feels considerable superiority because of her father's position. But as she grows older and demands are made upon her for real accomplishment the superior feeling disappears and she begins to question whether she can measure up to the family reputation. Convinced that she is the dumb one of the family, work does not bring the results which she desires. She begins to hide under the alibi, "Well, I don't care. I will not work any more. If I really worked I could be just as bright as the next one, but I don't intend to work." So she slips into a state of chronic laziness where she demands no effort from herself. It is a tremendous problem to restore in such a girl a sense of security and adequacy. Only through a slow, careful and patient technique can the reëstablishment of self-respect be made certain.

Every one dealing with adolescent girls is cognizant of the fact that the girl-boy relationship normally looms large upon the horizon and demands the most careful guidance. It is granted that this phase of development is as old as man himself; nevertheless, due to numerous factors which have entered into our civilization, the problems of this relationship to-day are relatively more acute and more complex. What difficult decisions these young people are called upon to make! Their physical development is urging the seeking of a mate but society and convention are demanding the learning of repression or sublimation of the sexual urge. Modern life is doing little to help but much to confuse these young people in reaching decisions. Through filmland all too frequently the ideals of love and of the beauty and sanctity of the home have been shattered for them at a very early age and no healthy substitutes have been put in their place. Through the influence of salacious literature which unfortunately is found in our so-called best homes and institutions of higher learning, obscene, indecent stories seem not at all incongruous to the ordinary conversation of mixed adolescent groups. Available to our youth has grown up a modern literature in which religion is ridiculed, the home is declared a failure, and free love is advocated as the means to mental health and happiness.

Added to these dangerous suggestions is the knowledge that devices of contraception, purchasable at any corner drug store, have brought about in women a change in attitude toward extramarital sex relations. In the quicksands of the confusion and complication of this free social organization the girls to-day are forced to gain a self-satisfying foothold.

Unfortunately the modern child does not follow the road nature has laid out for his development. Nature has wisely decreed that the transition from childhood into womanhood should be gradual. No child can mature overnight. It takes from four to five years—for a girl to become a woman. This is a physiologic law of growth. Our children skip from the mental and social age of twelve almost overnight to that of eighteen. Without possessing the restraining influence of adult judgment, they are thrown into the excitement and nervousness of adult life.[1]

It is not surprising that with no realization of her own lack of stability and control many a modern girl feels equal to any adventurous escapade and swept on by the mad, hectic speed of modern life declares that she wants not only to taste the cup of life's experiences but to drink even its dregs, that flippantly she bandies about hackneyed terms borrowed from popular literature, that she talks with sophistication about her philosophy of life, her determination to enjoy self-expression or sex expression, her disregard for authority, her utter disbelief in God. As one fifteen-year-old expressed it, "one must work from the customary atheism into a satisfying agnosticism." The seeming casualness of her acceptance of promiscuity and her declaration of the right to smoke, drink and "go

---

[1] Max Seham, *The Tired Child* (Philadelphia, J. B. Lippincott Co., 1926), pp. 297-320.

the limit" with her "boy-friend" make the need for guidance more necessary. Yet there are theorists who hail this day of sexual freedom as a mark of progress. It is encouraging to read the sane, wholesome refutation of the Freudian theory of repression of sexuality in the following excerpt by Dr. G. F. Morton: [2]

Whatever medical opinion may be, experience as a school master has led the writer to the conclusion that in youth it is sexual *expression* rather than *repression* which makes the neurotic character. The repression involved is that of moral demands. The libido, the psychic energy, fails to surmount one of the components of the infantile personality—the tendency to give in to oneself. The youth fails to adapt himself to the moral demands, i.e. to himself, since moral demands are a function of the human soul.

It seems wholly impossible to suppress these so-called heralds of the gospel of freedom, nor can we ever hope nor perhaps desire that youth be protected from all temptations and shielded from problems. The great challenge to educators is to guide and direct them during this normal period of development so that they will be strong enough to resist the quackery and shoddiness of some of our modern theories. Well might they profit by the philosophy of the Greeks of ancient days: "Nothing in excess."

Another problem familiar to all personnel workers is the necessary correction of wrong attitudes toward learning which are so prevalent in our schools.

A young person of fine intellectual attainment, a truly educated person, remarked recently, "During the last six

---

[2] G. F. Morton, *Childhood's Fears* (New York, The Macmillan Company, 1925), p. 91.

years I have been thrown into utter confusion about this thing called education. I went through high school blissfully unconscious of marks for we had no marks and I thought that I knew what it all meant. To my amazement, when I entered college I was led to believe that my high school experience had been all wrong. Professors and students alike talked of learning in terms of A's and B's. Thereupon, my whole method of attack was revolutionized and I started on the quest for grades. Incidently, I studied the whims and idiosyncrasies of my professors and I got my A's but at times the experience was galling. Now I am a college graduate and to my surprise I hear that the college admits that its former system was all wrong and is advocating mastery of material and elimination of grades. The thought came to me, 'Well, my high school was right after all and now they are getting together.' Not so—a visit to the high school brings the information that they have adopted the former attitude of the college and are now emphasizing grades and rank in class. It is queer, isn't it? What is this thing called education?"

These are the reflections of a mature, thinking student. Unfortunately, most of our pupils never stop to doubt or question because few ever have had the remotest conception of what eight years spent in high school and college should mean. Well developed "get-by" attitudes, cheating, working to satisfy a teacher, jealousy over marks attained by others, comparisons of class rating and standing are some of the glaring defects which point to lack of appreciation of the whole purpose of education. Studying and learning? What is the connotation to most pupils? Merely that they have satisfied an instructor by going through the motions of completing a certain number of assigned tasks in a given period of time and thereby, they have gained a credit toward graduation, fifteen of which credits mean the pupil is educated.

"Mr. ———— has failed me. I don't see why, I did everything he asked me to. I even attended opportunity class every night." A common example of this attitude. The fact that little knowledge was gained and limited understanding acquired never occurred to this pupil. Yet another common saying: "Mr. ———— is willing to give me my credit if you are." As if credits were commodities handed out by instructors much as an article of food is passed across a counter by a clerk.

Mary is told that she is not ready to graduate and pursue her studies in an institution of higher learning. The quick retort comes, "Why not? I have sixteen credits, haven't I?" Yes, she had sixteen units toward graduation but her record was a veritable patch-work quilt of half learning, three-quarters learning and in no case complete learning.

A great deal has been written about the relation of I.Q. to school success. No one works long with pupils without being convinced that not all failures occur among the pupils of low I.Q. nor are the outstanding scholastic successes among those of high I.Q. In a great many cases it seems to make little difference whether the pupil has an I.Q. of 110 or 142. The thing which does make for failure, mediocrity or success is whether the girl knows what she is about, whether she has sensed the purpose of our whole educative process or not. The girl with I.Q. 110 who has learned that education is her own personal development brought about by contact with and assimilation of the content of the various fields of knowledge will advance farther and become better educated than the brilliant, superior girl with I.Q. 142 who is still in the lesson-memorizing, lesson-reciting, mark-accumulating stage. One keen youngster well on the road to real learning said, "I flunked my ——— course but I learned more in that course than in any course I ever passed. I've learned to think and I don't believe that I can ever again swallow everything whole for I have begun to sense the need of discrimination." She bore the mark of school failure but she was in truth being educated and she was fully conscious of the fact.

The task of combating erroneous conceptions of learning is indeed a prodigious one because the roots of false theories go far down in the history of education. It is a slow, painful process to eradicate the all too common belief that learning is a set of facts poured in by some outside agent paid to mete out information in set doses, something to be memorized, parroted back at set intervals and to be forgotten as quickly as possible after the final examination.

What tremendous changes, what a balance and what an appreciation of values would appear in the student bodies of the high schools of this country if each pupil could be imbued with the truth and could grasp and accept the thought that true learning takes place within oneself and brings in its wake personal growth and maturity of action.

All too frequently parental attitudes create problems needlessly.

The overcompensating parent makes life a great burden for many adolescents and often jeopardizes their chances for success.

Mother was never good in school, in fact, she repeated the first year of high school and finally left in despair. At the age of forty her own failure to secure an education makes her persistency in forcing her daughter to go to school even greater. The latter must go to college, in fact, an eastern college. But the daughter does not learn readily, every course is difficult, soon she is out of her depth. It is futile to attempt to convince the mother that her offspring possesses just about the same traits and abilities which made it impossible for her in her youth to complete high school. The mother refuses to accept the facts. Her compensations take the form of complaints. The methods and policies of the school are all wrong, the teachers are antagonistic, refuse to give individual attention and never give a square deal. School interviews are repeated demonstrations of emotional upset. At home the defense is changed. Mother nags the girl, blames her for stupidity, inattention and carelessness, compares her with other members of the family or with the children of her friends. With sobs she cries that she is so disgraced that she cannot face her friends. As a result of such treatment at home and at school helplessness and discouragement characterize her daughter's attitude. Through these compensations for failure this type of mother makes an intolerable situation at home and at school.

Instructors are shocked yet mystified when Isabelle, who comes from a good home, one of culture and apparent refinement, says, "I want to leave this school and go as far away from home as possible. California would suit me best because I couldn't come home even at Christmas time." Our first reaction is: what an ingrate Isabelle is, how unfeeling and unappreciative! Every advantage known to parents has been given to her and yet she prefers to go so far away that she cannot be visited by her family nor can she visit them. What is the story? Antagonism! Not an uncommon state of affairs at all. In Isabelle's home the antagonism had been of slow growth and of long standing. The personnel worker had Isabelle under her supervision for many years and saw her go through the most exasperating home situations. During her first year in high school the teachers were constantly sending her to the office for impertinence, loudness, swearing and every form of exhibitionism. One had only to go down the school corridor once a day to know that Isabelle was compensating, getting rid of excess steam and trying to convince everybody together with herself that she was a somebody. Often upon her entrance into a classroom she would almost shout, "Well, here I am!"

A visit to her home made it possible to understand very clearly what Isabelle constantly complained of, her "family tree." In order to appreciate the charged atmosphere of that household one must go back to the maternal grandmother who is still a member of the group. Grandma had been raised in a quiet, retiring Quaker family which lived in the country. Her parents were strict and firm. At a very early age grandmother married a dashing young man from a big eastern city. His family were prominent people. They were among the "best families." Grandmother expanded accordingly but in six years she sought divorce because her husband was unfaithful. There was only one child, Isabelle's mother. The grandmother being deprived of her husband's affection lavished everything on her child. She spoiled her;

she made her feel that the whole world should bow at her feet—in fact, that she was the center of the universe. At eighteen Isabelle's mother married a handsome young man of great wealth after six weeks' acquaintance. Pampered and spoiled, she whined if she were crossed in any respect. Isabelle was born. Instead of making a real woman out of the mother, it made her jealous of the baby in her husband's affection, and she became suspicious of him. When Isabelle was five years old divorce proceedings started. During the next six years Isabelle's mother went through a fortune and married again. This time she married a cynical, dominating, opinionated man who had never grown up emotionally. He, too, was a spoiled only child. Such is the family background: A grandmother who still lives in the light of her social prominence thirty-eight years ago; a mother, neurotic, whining and jealous, Isabelle another only child, and a stepfather. All the adults of the household dictate to and nag Isabelle. The mother is jealous of the relationship between Isabelle and the stepfather, the stepfather is very fond of Isabelle but he cannot show even interest in her progress without creating a scene. Being a weak, spoiled individual himself when things get too exasperating he literally "blows up." He dare not strike the grandmother nor his wife so he gets emotional relief by slapping Isabelle. The mother constantly harps on her own unselfishness in Isabelle's behalf. The new dress is bought not for herself but for Isabelle. But as Isabelle says, "I have to listen for a month to complaints of how little I appreciate all the sacrifice until I wish I had never had a new dress, in fact, I never wanted it in the first place. My mother would buy it in spite of all my protests." So we see the mother getting *selfish satisfaction* out of what she would call *unselfishness*. This tale of antagonism could be drawn out indefinitely. And yet the world expects Isabelle, the victim of it all, to be emotionally normal. Is it surprising that she is the last girl to leave school at night because she hates to go home, that she is seen and heard all day long and that she wants to get as far away from home as possible? The wonder of it is that Isabelle ranks scholastically rather high and is quite normal in most of her ideas except marriage.

Mabel was a brilliant, retiring student at school but was reported to be a disagreeable girl in the home. Charges of impertinence, arrogance and disobedience to her father were made. The case was brought into the school by the mother to see if help could be given. After much investigation it came to light that the father was terrifically jealous of Mabel for her excellent school record. He had always wanted to graduate from high school but economic conditions had thwarted his ambition. Mabel had advanced far beyond him in actual book learning and he could not suppress his own "ego" sufficiently to get enjoyment out of her success. He felt that he had to dominate her to keep his own self-respect. His actions went to the most absurd lengths. For example, it is, without a doubt, the consensus of opinion that the traffic signals are green, yellow and red yet Mabel in her home was never permitted to speak of the green light because her father said the light was blue, so "blue" it had to be. All the friction in the home, Mabel's tantrums and the serious rebellions could be traced to some trifling, irritating experience such as the above. The fact that Mabel had forgotten to wear rubbers to school when her father had casually suggested it could plunge the whole family into civil war for days.

In the same way in which many people resort to quackery in medicine, or become advocates of every new cult which appears or swear by popular patent medicines so it is becoming increasingly common that some parents are showing a "flair for psychiatry."

Dr. Joseph Brenneman says: "Baffling problems are being created by parents who are the victims of the wholesale education of the laity in all that pertains to child study, guidance and training; in parent education; in child psychology; psychiatry, behaviorism and even in psychoanalysis of different brands." [3]

In school work it is evident that many intelligent parents have been carried away by the wave of popular psychiatry so that half truths and half knowledge are playing havoc with home attitudes. In some localities it has spread like a communicable disease. The reading of a popular treatment of adolescent behavior or attendance at one or two lectures on psychoanalysis can so distort the perspective of these parents that they lose their normal outlook and have no sense of proportion. Reactions in the home are put under the microscope; actions and attitudes are misconstrued, and normal behavior is misinterpreted as serious problems.

Examples are legion. One or two cases will suffice to clarify the point. Bessie was a quiet, unassuming, quite mature youngster of thirteen. She always exhibited fineness of taste and was an interested member of a class group. Although her social contacts were few and she

---

[3] Joseph Brenneman, "The Menace of Psychiatry," *American Journal of Diseases of Children,* August, 1931 (Vol. 42), pp. 376-402.

participated only occasionally in group activity, the fact remained that her contacts were satisfying, and non-participation was not a source of annoyance. Bessie's mother, a vivid person, vivacious, loquacious and socially prominent, could never comprehend that Bessie in her quiet, self-effacing, poised way, was perfectly happy and contented. She was determined that Bessie should be different. The "unsocial child" was the label by which she tagged Bessie. No book or magazine in which the unsocial child was discussed was overlooked. The merest inkling of a meeting where there might be the possibility of a discussion would send her feverishly on her way. The answer was going to be found if it were humanly possible. At the school, too, she sought help. During the interview the truth came out. Bessie was exactly like her father and his side of the house. With the force of an invective the mother hurled the statement, "She shall not be like her Aunt Gertrude!" Advice was given to let Bessie alone. This, however, was interpreted as inefficiency, lack of foresight and no sympathy with problems of such a nature. The advice went unheeded and the quest continued.

Next came a request that Bessie be excused to leave school for three or four hours so that a famous psychiatrist might be consulted. Permission was granted but Bessie not only refused to go but showed genuine resentment toward her mother at the whole idea. Quite out of keeping with her usual calmness, she vociferously asserted, "I'm no problem. The problem is all in my mother's head. I see no reason to go to a psychiatrist. She can't make me like herself. I hate her constant talking and her *social* attitude. I'm like my father and I want to be like

BIBLIOGRAPHY

ADDAMS, Jane, *et al.*, *The Child, the Clinic and the Court* (New York, New Republic Publishing Co., 1925.

ADLER, Alfred, *et al.*, *Guiding the Child* (New York, Greenberg, Publisher, Inc., 1930).

ALLPORT, Floyd, *Social Psychology* (Boston, Houghton Mifflin Co., 1924).

BENEDICT, Agnes E., *Children at the Crossroads* (New York, The Commonwealth Fund, 1930).

BLANCHARD, Phyllis, *The Adolescent Girl* (New York, Dodd, Mead & Co., 1924).

——— *The Child and Society* (New York, Longmans Green & Co., 1928).

BLANCHARD, Phyllis and MANASSES, C., *New Girls for Old* (New York, Macaulay Co., 1930).

BRAM, Israel, *Goiter: Non-Surgical Types and Treatment* (New York, Macmillan Co., 1924).

BRONNER, A. F., HEALY, William, LOWE, G. M. and SHIMBERG, M. E., *A Manual of Individual Tests and Testing* (Boston, Little, Brown & Co., 1927).

BROOKS, F. D., *Psychology of Adolescence* (Boston, Houghton Mifflin Co., 1929).

BURNHAM, William H., *The Normal Mind* (New York, D. Appleton & Co., 1924).

——— *The Wholesome Personality* (New York, D. Appleton & Co., 1932).

BURT, Cyril L., *The Young Delinquent* (New York, D. Appleton & Co., 1925).

CAHILL, Beatrice H., *Pupil Guidance* (Boston, Colonial Press, 1929).

DORSEY, George Amos, *Hows and Whys of Human Behavior* (New York, Harper & Bros., 1929).

ELLIOTT, Grace L., *Understanding the Adolescent Girl* (New York, Henry Holt & Co., 1929).

EMERSON, William R., *Nutrition and Growth in Children* (New York, D. Appleton & Co., 1926).

———— *The Diagnosis of Health* (New York, D. Appleton & Co., 1930).

FISHBACK, HOLT and KIRKPATRICK, *Conduct Problems for Junior High School Grades* (Boston, D. C. Heath & Co., 1930).

FISHBACK, E. H., *Character Education in the Junior High School* (Boston, D. C. Heath & Co., 1928).

FREEMAN, Frank N., *Mental Tests* (Boston, Houghton Mifflin Co., 1926).

FRETWELL, Elbert K., *Extra-Curricular Activities in Secondary Schools* (Boston, Houghton Mifflin Co., 1931).

GERMANE, C. E. and GERMANE, E. G., *Character Education* (Newark, Silver, Burdett & Co., 1929).

GODDARD, H. H., *Feeble-Mindedness: Its Causes and Consequences* (New York, Macmillan Co., 1914).

GROVES, Ernest R., *Personality and Social Adjustment* (New York, Longmans, Green & Co., 1925).

HAGGARD, Howard W., *What You Should Know About Health and Disease* (New York, Harper & Bros., 1928).

HALL, G. Stanley, *Adolescence* (New York, D. Appleton & Co., 1905).

———— *Youth* (New York, D. Appleton & Co., 1906).

HARTSHORNE and MAY, *Studies in the Organization of Character* (New York, Macmillan Co., 1930).

HEALY, William, *The Structure and Meaning of Psychoanalysis as Related to Personality and Behavior* (New York, A. A. Knopf, 1930).

———— *Reconstructing Behavior in Youth* (New York, A. A. Knopf, 1929).

HOLLINGWORTH, Leta S., *Psychology of the Adolescent* (New York, D. Appleton & Co., 1928).

INSKEEP, Annie D., *Teaching Dull and Retarded Children* (New York, Macmillan Co., 1926).

———— *Child Adjustment in Relation to Growth and Development* (New York, D. Appleton & Co., 1930).

JACKSON, Arnold S., *Goiter and Other Diseases of the Thyroid Gland* (New York, Paul B. Hoeber, Inc., 1926).

JONES, A. J., *Principles of Guidance* (New York, McGraw-Hill Book Co., 1930).

Koos, L. V. and Kefauver, A. N., *Guidance in Secondary Schools* (New York, Macmillan Co., 1932).

Kuhlmann, F., *Handbook of Mental Tests* (Baltimore, Warwick & York, 1922).

La Rue, Daniel, *Mental Hygiene* (New York, Macmillan Co., 1928).

Leary, D. B., *Modern Psychology* (Philadelphia, J. B. Lippincott Co., 1928).

Lee, P. R. and Kenworthy, M. E., *Mental Hygiene and Social Work* (New York, The Commonwealth Fund, 1929).

Mateer, Florence, *The Unstable Child* (New York, D. Appleton & Co., 1924).

—— *Just Normal Children* (New York, D. Appleton & Co., 1929).

McDougall, William, *Character and the Conduct of Life* (New York, G. P. Putnam & Sons, 1927).

Morgan, J. J. B., *The Psychology of the Unadjusted School Child* (New York, Macmillan Co., 1924).

Morrison, H. C., *The Practice of Teaching in the Secondary School* (Chicago, University of Chicago Press, second edition, 1931), Chapter xxxi.

Mosher, C. D., *Personal Hygiene for Women* (Stanford University, Stanford University Press, 1927).

Mudge, H. L., *Varieties of Adolescent Experience* (New York, Century Co., 1926).

Olson, Willard C., *Measurement of Nervous Habits in Normal Children* (Minneapolis, University of Minnesota, 1929).

Overstreet, H. A., *About Ourselves* (New York, W. W. Norton & Co., 1927).

Paynter, R. H. and Blanchard, P., *Educational Achievement of Problem Children* (New York, The Commonwealth Fund, 1929).

Pierce, Anna Eloise, *Catalog of Student Health Literature* (Washington, D. C., National Association of Deans of Women, 1927).

Proceedings of the Mid-West Conference on Character Development, "The Child's Emotions" (Chicago, University of Chicago Press, 1930).

Rank, O., *Nervous and Mental Diseases*, Monograph Series, No. 18.

Reavis, W. C., *Pupil Adjustment* (New York, D. C. Heath & Co., 1926).

Richmond, Winifred, *The Adolescent Girl* (New York, Macmillan Co., 1925).

SADLER, W. S., *Piloting Modern Youth* (New York, Funk & Wagnalls, 1931).

SAYLES, Mary B., *The Problem Child At Home*, 1928; *The Problem Child In School*, 1925 (New York, The Commonwealth Fund).

TERMAN, Lewis M., *Mental and Physical Traits of 1000 Gifted Children* (Stanford University, Stanford University Press, 1925).

THOM, Douglas, *Everyday Problems of the Everyday Child* (New York, D. Appleton & Co., 1928).

—— *Normal Youth and Its Everyday Problems* (New York, D. Appleton & Co., 1932).

THOMAS, Dorothy S., *et al.*, *Some New Techniques for Studying Social Behavior*, Child Development Monographs (New York, Teachers College, Columbia University, 1929).

THOMAS, W. I., *The Unadjusted Girl* (Boston, Little, Brown & Co. 1927).

TRACY, Frederick, *Psychology of Adolescence* (New York, Macmillan Co., 1927).

TRAVIS, Thomas, *The Young Malefactor* (New York, T. W. Crowell & Co., 1908).

TREDGOLD, A. F., *Mental Deficiency* (New York, Wm. Wood & Co., 1929).

VALENTINE, P. F., *The Psychology of Personality* (New York, D. Appleton & Co., 1927).

VAN WATERS, Miriam, *Youth in Conflict* (New York, New Republic Publishing Co., 1925).

—— *Parents on Probation* (New York, New Republic Publishing Co., 1927).

WALLIN, J. E. W., *Clinical and Abnormal Psychology* (Boston, Houghton Mifflin Co., 1927).

WEMBRIDGE, Eleanor, *Other People's Daughters* (Boston, Houghton Mifflin Co., 1926).

—— *Life Among the Low Brows* (New York, Macmillan Co., 1931).

WICKMAN, E. K., *Children's Behavior and Teachers' Attitudes* (New York, The Commonwealth Fund, 1928).

WHITE, W. W., *Mechanisms of Character Formation* (New York, Macmillan Co., 1926).

WILLIAMS, Frankwood, *Adolescence* (New York, Farrar & Rinehart, 1930).

WOODROW, H. H., *Brightness and Dullness in Children* (Philadelphia, J. B. Lippincott Co., 1919).

WÒOLLEY, Helen Thompson, *An Experimental Study of Children* (New York, Macmillan Co., 1926).

ZACHRY, Caroline B., *Personality Adjustments of School Children* (New York, Chas. Scribner's Sons, 1929).

INDEX

(1)

WIT'DRAWN